OVER-EXTENSION UNIVERSITY BULLETIN

School of Continual Education and Self-Enlargement

GERALD SUSSMAN, DEAN

M. Evans and Co., Inc.   New York

Acknolwedgments

I would like to thank my editor Fred Graver for his strong support and invaluable editing skill. And a special thanks to my fashion stylists, Elaine Louie and Patricia Ashley.

Library of Congress Cataloging in Publication Data

Sussman, Gerald.
  Over-extension university bulletin.

  1. Continuing education—Curricula—Anecdotes, facetiae, satire, etc. 2. Life skills—Anecdotes, facetiae, satire, etc. I. Title.
LC5219.S9   1982   374   82-13860

ISBN 0-87131-389-8

Copyright © 1982 by Gerald Sussman

All rights reserved. No part of this book may be reproduced or transmitted in any form or by any means without the written permission of the publisher.

M. Evans and Company, Inc.
216 East 49 Street
New York, New York 10017

Design by RFS Graphic Design, Inc.

Photographs of Over-Extension University by Tom Conroy (Movie Archives)

Manufactured in the United States of America

9 8 7 6 5 4 3 2 1

OVER-EXTENSION UNIVERSITY BULLETIN

INTRODUCTORY MESSAGE FROM THE DEAN

Welcome to Over-Extension University.

It is my pleasure to welcome you to this great university of self-enlargement and continual education. Though it is comparitively new (founded in 1982), it is dedicated to the ancient tradition of great universities everywhere—the tradition of offering you the finest and most useful knowledge available.

Along with our ancient traditions we are also dedicated to the future—*your* future. Our goals coincide with your goals—to give you the kind of education that will make you a successful, charismatic person, enhance the quality of your lifestyle and enable you to find a new lover.

Our instructors are gifted professionals who give freely of themselves, both intellectually and physically. Our relaxed, highly adult atmosphere will stimulate you to learn hundreds of new and exciting subjects, develop new friendships, make new professional and business contacts to advance your career and find a new lover.

I'm sure that Over-Extension will be your first choice because dollar for dollar, course for course, it's the best educational value in the country. *With the cost of education what it is today you simply can't afford not to enroll with us.* Besides the low, low tuition fees we also offer inexpensive group rates, discounts to union members and other recognized groups, special rates to senior citizens and the incredible charter membership in our Golden Lifetime Student Plan.

How do we do it? We operate at staggering losses. Over-Extension University is a tax shelter and write-off for a very large, prestigious conglomerate that decided to endow an entire university with the premise that the school would offer their courses at fees "below wholesale."

I'm confident you will find Over-Extension University the one school of continual education that will fulfill your hopes, dreams and aspirations and make you a stand-out person. And most important, OU is the only school in the country with a *money-back guarantee* if you do not find a new lover.

Sincerely,

Gerald Sussman, Dean

A BRIEF HISTORY OF THE SCHOOL

Over-Extension University was founded in September 1982 by Gerald Sussman, in partnership with MelSidMac Modes, a division of Hy-Jay Enterprises, part of Spittsbard Industries, a wholly-owned subsidiary of A.G. Grunefarbescheit of Basel. It is approved by the State Board of Regents and all veterans groups and is legally registered in Manila. The official mascot of Over-Extension University is the marmoset and its colors are hot pink and Granny Smith green.

A GUIDE TO THE BULLETIN

EVERYTHING YOU WANT TO KNOW ABOUT OUR SCHOOL

- If you need advice on any course, see counselors Rhoda Skorn or Tyler Moleman, who are often using the public phones on the main floor in the rear, every evening but Thursday.

- If you're exploring new career opportunities and need help, attend our weekly Resume Planning Seminar in the basement. Free Perrier and fish chips.

- If you're interested in degrees, certificates, diplomas, sheepskins or other official acknowledgments of your work, see Mr. Henry Gomma in room 234 for special discount prices.

- If you want to use any of the courses as credit toward regular undergraduate or graduate school requirements, see Mr. Anthony Calzone in room 624. Mr. Calzone does excellent work in modifying and adapting transcripts at very reasonable prices.

- If math is your problem and you are interested in overcoming Math Anxiety, see Miss Arlette in the East Wing annex, room C.

- If you're a veteran of any war or have seen some kind of military or para-military service, or have been a Boy Scout, Girl Scout or belong to any qualified business or fraternal organization, see Mr. Joel Trembler in room 567 or 568 for a package deal or special courtesy discount.

- If you do not have a high school or high school equivalency diploma, don't worry about it.

- If you are specially interested in our Social Adventure courses, see Mr. Johnny Suavino or Miss Donna DiMoona in room 300. They will help you plan the courses just right for your specific needs.

- If, God forbid, you pass away while attending any of our classes you can be covered by purchasing a very inexpensive life insurance policy from Mr. Teddy LaBonz in room 439.

- If you need special financial aid for a specific course or full program, see Mr. Carmine Coozio in the back room of Pepi's Lounge, two blocks south of the school.

- If English is not your first language but you still want to "sit in" on some of our courses, see Mr. Irving Fliegel for a special price.

- If you're interested in meeting a particular instructor after classes, see Mr. Carl Mink in room 457 for more details.
- If you're interested in joining our auxiliary Health and Racquet Club, see Miss Nina Scopitone, room 101, for our very attractive introductory rates.
- If you wish to obtain an OU ID card which is essential for admittance to weekend classes, see Al in our souvenir shop in the main lobby.
- If you need any books, magazines or other study material relating to your courses, don't buy anything in a regular bookstore until you see Vinnie, in the basement, room J, for special prices.
- When you meet your new lover in one of your courses and want to dine out in the vicinity, see Mr. Sal Vendetta for special discount parking coupons.
- If you need a key to the men's or ladies' rooms submit a request in writing to Margaret Romanza, room 404, along with 75¢ to cover the cost of the key.
- If you're terribly frightened of going back to school and ashamed of exposing your ignorance to a classroom of students, attend our free Awkward, Shy, and Stupid Seminar, every Wednesday evening at 11:45 PM in room 290.

HOW TO REGISTER

- There is a registration fee of $1.50 for each course, which is nonrefundable.
- Students can register at the school at any time of day or night. If you register in person, ask for Estelle, Alice or Betty in the Registration Office, room 109.
- If you are registering by mail, send us your name, address and what courses you want. You can pay for the courses by check, money order, travelers check, bank check or stamps.

If you're more comfortable sending cash, by all means send it. Please wrap the cash carefully in two hankies before you put it in the envelope.

WE ACCEPT ALL DOMESTIC AND FOREIGN CREDIT CARDS

- If you're registering by phone, call one of our toll-free numbers (800-999-9999). Our courteous operators are on duty 24 hours a day. If the lines are busy, please be patient.
- If you need a receipt for your tuition payment, see Miss Josephine LaBomba in room 278.

- There is no such thing as a class that is *filled* at Over-Extension University. There is always room for another student. Just tell us what course you want and we'll make sure you get it.

OVER-EXTENSION UNIVERSITY BULLETIN

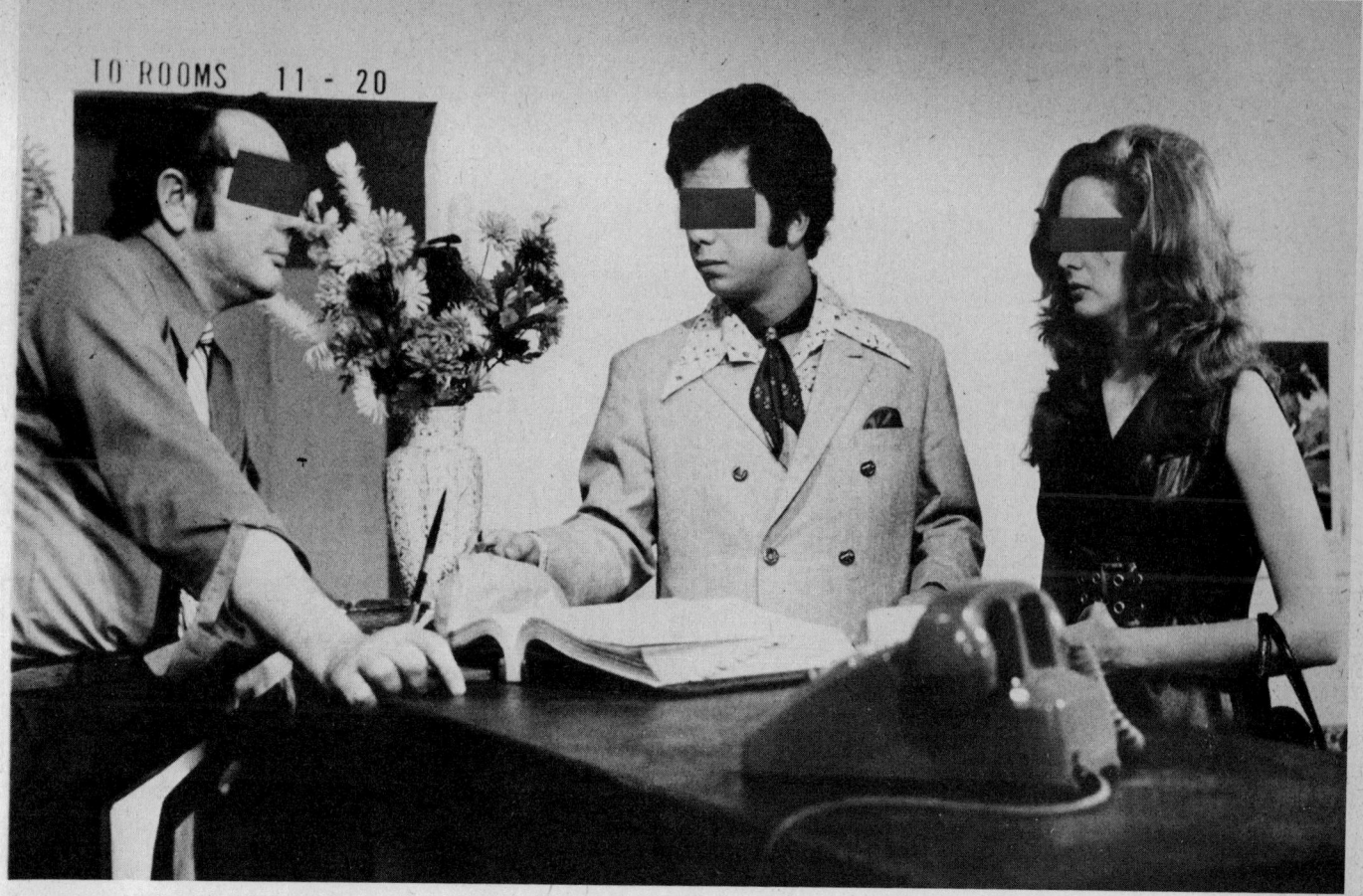

CAREERS

#11743—FLOPHOUSE AND LOVE HOTEL MANAGEMENT
(Thurs., 7:30, $20)
Norman Turlman

Two of the fastest-growing segments of the hostelry business are flophouses and love hotels. Though not as glamorous and well-publicized as the more legitimate parts of the industry, they have enjoyed remarkable growth in the past few years. Both flophouses and love hotels are designed for minimum overhead and high turnover, producing enormous profits. Both operations can be run with a small, low-paid staff.

Mr. Turlman will discuss the advantages of these businesses and how you can break into management and eventual ownership. He will show you how to increase the profit potential of a flophouse with sex-aid vending machines, minimum laundry service and extra charges for "options" such as towels, soap and blankets.

The love hotel, designed for quick assignations, offers even greater profit potential, with many of its rooms rented in hourly shifts. Mr. Turlman will analyze the most critical problem in love hotel management—linens.

The high costs of laundering in a love hotel can cut into the profits. Rather than becoming a victim of the commercial laundry monopolies, Mr. Turlman advances the notion of returning to the old fashioned "Ma and Pa" approach. That is, doing the laundry yourself in a basement washing machine or at a nearby laundromat. He proposes a simple effective wash-dry-iron method and bed make-up system that can be handled with a small, well-disciplined staff. "A good profitable love hotel should be as much a vertical operation as possible," says Mr. Turlman.

Mr. Turlman will take his students on field trips to some of the more successful flophouses and love hotels in the area where you can observe the actual operations and have all your questions answered by the highly qualified professional management.

#99950—GAYS IN COMPUTER PROGRAMMING
A Career Crisis Workshop
(9:00, May 20, $60)
Marc Winslow

The popular image that most gays have managed to create for themselves is that of a highly organized, extremely neat and precise person who is very good at formal logic. These qualities make them the ideal type of personnel for computer programming, and in fact, many Gays are drawn into this highly lucrative field.

Unfortunately, new studies have proven that many Gays are *not* by temperament suited to their work in computer programming and are having great difficulty in adjusting and living up to their popular image. This workshop will explore the image crisis of Gays in this

Careers 7

area, how the image was wrongly conceived by the straight population, how the first Gays in computer programming reacted and went along with the misconceptions in order to keep their jobs, and most important, how Gays can overcome this false myth and still maintain and improve their positions.

#57936—BROILING AND TOASTING FRANCHISES
How to Get in on the Ground Floor of a Hot New Service Industry
(Mon., 9:00, $25)
Lew Masterson

For many of today's rising young executives, the idea of cooking has become a dreaded chore—a time-consuming, baffling activity that has driven many of them into eating out virtually every night, a costly alternative.

If you've ever tried to toast a fat bagel in the thin opening of a toaster, or attempted to broil a perfect steak, you can appreciate the difficulties which are producing this substantial new market. Many investment analysts and trend spotters agree that the answer to the acute problems of the noncook is the growing new broiling and toasting industry, or B 'n' T Franchises.

Now more than ever, the time and patience needed to develop the skills of toasting and broiling are in short supply. It has been discovered that many will pay to have the services of a professional toaster and broiler. Toasting and broiling have evolved into highly specialized operations.

The B 'n' T operation offers simple, quickly prepared food for the busy "I Hate to Cook" person. It is *not* a total cooking service, offering the only two cooking activities deemed essential by most people in this market. The service can be bought with or without the customer's own food, or chew-ware, as it is called. Every conceivable type of toasting and broiling is done on the consumer's premises with B 'n' T equipment, from breakfast muffins to grilled sandwiches and broiled meats, fowl and fish.

The B 'n' T concept started a few years ago on the West Coast with the Popsizzle and CharToast chains. Both companies plan to "roll out" and go nationwide in the near future. Many other regional B 'n' T franchise chains will soon follow.

Lew Masterson, who has worked for both Popsizzle and CharToast, offers an insightful look at the rewards and the risks involved in this volatile new industry. He will discuss how you lease your equipment, how to set up your home service system, how to create a menu (with and without your own chew-ware), sales methods, promotions, advertising and marketing of the B 'n' T concept.

#63478—BECOME AN EMERGENCY PARA-PSYCHOLOGIST
(Tues., 7:30, $15)
Bruce Dimpler, B.S.

One of the fastest growing new careers in the country, para-psychology requires no formal degree (although we do issue a handsomely engraved certificate and an authentic ID badge). If you have the need and willingness to help total strangers, the ability to be a good listener and the skill to extract a fee for your services you can become a successful para-psychologist.

There are millions of people walking the streets today who need some kind of psychiatric help. Some people won't admit that they need it. Most people cannot afford it. Yet we can see the unmistakable look on their faces, a look of despair, frustration, anxiety or boredom, a look that says, "I know I'm not perfect. I have problems that I can't solve by myself. I really could use a little professional or even semi-professional help."

The role of the para-psychologist is to seek out these people and offer emergency consultation. Bruce Dimpler (see faculty index), who once majored in psychology, will teach you how to spot people with problems, how to convince a potential patient that he needs help and, of course, how to psychoanalyze and cure the patient quickly and painlessly right on the spot.

The para-psychologist will be given an intense briefing in psychoanalytical techniques using Mr. Dimpler's patented "psycho shortcuts" which distill the essentials of analysis into three basic ills which require three basic cures. In conclusion, the para-psychologist will be trained in the most effective methods of obtaining a fee for his services. (Early practitioners of para-psychology were usually given an appropriate pat on the back, a kiss on the cheek or a "let's have lunch or let me buy you a drink" kind of compensation.) Today's para-psychologist must be taught how to extract quick payments and, if necessary, how to use a computer-controlled billing system.

Para-psychology is not intended to be a definitive cure for profound emotional problems. A wise bit of advice to all patients is: "If pain persists, see your doctor . . . if you can afford one." But a good para-psychologist will offer temporary relief to simple problems and give a troubled person the encouragement and incentive to become a genuine psychiatric patient someday.

#00001—HOW TO START A TINY BUSINESS
(Thurs., 9:00, $30)
Armand Von Limbo

Many businessmen have created a pattern of failure and self-destructiveness in their ventures that they refuse to recognize, and yet they persist in their fruitless quests for success. The reason they fail is simple: they have cultivated a delusion of grandeur, a monstrous ego that has been fed by a lifelong need to overreach, overachieve and climb recklessly up the ladder of success at any cost to themselves and others. They fail to become millionaires or earn even a fraction of that amount. And the toll of these failed businessmen is becoming distressingly higher.

Armand Von Limbo, author of *Small Is Beautiful, But Tiny Is Terrific*, offers the only realistic alternative to the failed overachiever—the very small business that can be developed and managed to perfection without driving him to a nervous breakdown.

"Start tiny and stay tiny," says Von Limbo. As a classic example, he shows you how to create a lemonade stand. If the urge to expand is too great, he shows how to add a shoeshine stand (one box) and a newspaper route.

Other tiny ventures you can develop are the "Loose Businesses": selling loose Q-Tips (to relieve sudden ear itch), selling loose flower and vegetable seeds, cuff links, odd buttons and other tiny items you can store in your pockets. You can create your own tiny service industry such as Cigarette Lighting (for the heavy smoker). This can be combined with selling loose tissues to relieve smoker's cough. Another booming service industry is selling scented towelettes to people whose faces perspire heavily in hot weather. You'll learn how to set up your "stand" right in the elevator of a large office building, so your customers can freshen up as they return from lunch.

All these businesses and many more are easy to learn and require little overhead. Though they may offer only a modest income they more than make up for it by keeping you well within your natural limitations and rewarding you with a prize that is worth more than a million dollars—your health. Armand Von Limbo will help you save your life as he teaches you to stay tiny, rather than burning yourself out and dying of a heart attack at an early age in the effort to achieve what is clearly beyond your ability.

#53679—WRITE AND PERISH!
How to Be a Starving Fiction Writer
(Wed., 9:00, $20)
Steven Menschevik

Eugene O'Neill, Ernest Hemingway, Thomas Wolfe—were all once starving writers, unable to sell a scrap of their work, as they decorated their bleak garrets with pink rejection slips. And then they turned the corner, became successful and drove themselves to tragedy and ruin. In contrast to these artists, consider Jack Frasker, Neville Schinto and William Rayon—they too began as starving, unsuccessful writers. But they stuck to their ideals, clung to their way of life and never had to struggle with the insolvable, fatal problem of success.

The secret of becoming a starving writer is simple—write uncommercial material, material that only you and perhaps a handful of chosen, lucky people believe in. You do not have to be inherently talented. A stubbornly uncommercial streak, combined with the ability to pour words on paper are all that is needed. (If you are not prolific and hard working and want to become a writer manqué, a pseudo intellectual or a poseur, please be patient. A new course in this highly popular alternative field is being prepared for next semester. Our current course is for the more dedicated artist.)

As a starving artist, you will have the gut feeling of knowing that you are living a life of pure integrity, being true to yourself and your vision, no matter how many hardships you have to endure. You may go to bed hungry and lonely, but deep down inside you are happier than the man who has sold out, who has compromised his life and lives in a dull, deadly world of underachievement, boredom and frustration. Whether you are living off a meager little income and devoting your entire life to writing, or working at another job to pay your expenses so you can write in your spare time, you will learn how to enjoy the fruits of poverty and the life of an unsuccessful artist.

The first section of the course deals with the forms of uncommercial fiction and the novel—or more specifically, "the first novel." Steven Menschevik, author of thirty-seven unpublished novels, will share with you what he describes as "the best years of my life . . . my starving years" as he guides you into this fascinating, romantic and emotionally rewarding way of life.

Examples of the uncommercial first novel include: the Joycean proletarian novel, the spy or mystery thriller written in verse, the novel about Third World problems, novels about eccentric old women living in small towns, novels about poor, underprivileged minorities living in big cities, novels exposing the grim world of iron miners, novels of the seafaring life, any novel that experiments with language, structure and time, novels about boredom and ennui and long, dense autobiographical novels in the form of diaries and journals. Mr. Menschevik will also discuss the short story ("a one way ticket to nowhere"), the novella ("a forgotten form that will never come back") and poetry ("an academic exercise that belongs in Academe").

Dedication to the uncommercial style has its pitfalls, as well. "You will be tempted to create characters that are *likable*," Mr. Menschevik counsels, "or narratives that are *easy to follow*—if only for your own convenience. Most of all, you must fight the urge to rewrite, even when you are tempting to make your work *more* uncommercial. Rule number one: The first draft is the most *true*."

You will also learn techniques of survival as a starving writer. How to sponge off richer people, how to become an appealing drunk, how to maintain an attractively arrogant, stubbornly idealistic yet vulnerable persona, how to get people to empathize and help you and how to attract women and live off them. You will also learn desperation survival techniques such as stealing, check forging, low-budget cooking and fraudulent blood donating.

Along with Mr. Menschevik, we will present special guest lecturers, the Black novelist Lonny Chitling, author of sixty-three unpublished novels including *Native Daughter* and *Invisible Woman*, Abraham Kashruth, author of such unknown books as *The Drapes of Roth*, the Studs Lefcowitz trilogy and *Goldie's Choice*, and James Updown, whose unpublished works include *Bunny Run*, *Bunny Redeux* and *Bunny Is Rich*.

#3979—BEGGING: HIGH INCOME WITH LOW OVERHEAD
(Wed., 8:30, whatever you can spare)
Tommy O'Callaghan

The old saying "Beggars can't be choosers" is certainly outdated and untrue if you are considering begging as a career. To the contrary, there is now a greater choice of jobs in this field than ever before. To keep this vocation in proper perspective it is important to remember that in many countries begging is not considered a pitiful way of life but rather an ancient and honorable family tradition which is passed on for generations.

Begging offers you the chance for a high income at little cost, using just a little

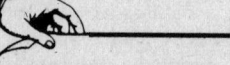

● **SPECIAL HUMANITIES OFFER** ●

Get two courses for the price of one, three for the price of two. See Estelle, room 205.

ingenuity on your part. And most importantly, all your income is tax free.

Tommy O'Callaghan has been a successful beggar for over forty years, working in many styles and many cities across the country. Along with our guest lecturers he will help you create your own personal begging style. There is only one prerequisite for being a good beggar: You must be an inherently good actor, and a "nervy" person. You must create a role, a style for yourself. It is virtually impossible to be a successful beggar if you are shy, diffident, lack confidence and cannot communicate with your potential contributors.

Here are some of the begging styles and techniques that will be covered:

1. *The sincere, disheveled, ragged, disgusting look.* You simply ask for money with a genuinely humble look ("please, anything you can spare . . ."). You look awful. You wear "dirty makeup" and smell rotten. Wardrobe is important. Wear shoes made of newspaper, a coat that looks like it's made of a rope doormat. A weeks' worth of facial stubble is good. The overall effect is a total degradation. The physical, visual qualities are more important than what you say in your "pitch."
2. *Sincere, moderately well-dressed look*. This style requires very little wardrobe change or makeup but is far more difficult to use, unless you are a consummate actor. One method is to simply stand in front of a subway entrance and ask people for a small sum to get you on the train ("a few cents to make the fare"). You look reasonably respectable but just a bit down on your luck. Perhaps you lost your wallet. The main thing to convey is that you just need a nickel, dime, quarter to pay for a token. This sounds easy, looks easy, but actually needs a special kind of sincerity, persistence, confidence, and the motivation to get dressed for work.
3. *The threatening look.* People of any size can pose a physical threat, and this method teaches you how to look, act, and talk dangerously while asking for money. You'll learn the "Seven Ominous Signs" of impending violence, and how to put them to work as a beggar.

Our special guest lecturers will deal with many other fields. Josh Kronenfelder will show you how to become a successful activist beggar, specializing in fake environmental and anti-establishment causes, using fake petitions and a small coffee mug. Mr. O'Callaghan will show you how to sell fake church raffle tickets and other charity scams. You can elect to go into the service divisions of begging, such as cleaning windshields at stoplights, or quick shoeshines.

Traditional modes of begging will be analyzed. You'll find out how to look handicapped, fake blindness, deafness and dumbness . . . with or without a Seeing Eye dog. If you have the energy and inclination, you can learn to be a successful whiner and screamer, suffering from an incurable disease.

Practical aspects of begging, such as choosing locations, self-protection, and how to handle cash will be discussed, as well as bribing local police, competition from rivals, wardrobe, makeup and budget hints.

Note: Our teachers are true professionals and expect a reasonable "contribution" from their students after each session.

#65213—CAREER OPPORTUNITIES IN CABLE
(Fri., 7:30, $30)
Henry C. Tonnaway

There is no question that one of the major career opportunities of the 80s will be in cable. In virtually every business and industry, cable plays a vital role—whether in telephone systems, electrical lines or in its related forms, heavy-duty wire and cord.

The hows and whys of cable technology will be explored and analyzed by various experts, with discussions of the newest cable materials and their characteristics. Guest engineers will demonstrate the versatility and stress characteristics of cable and wire. Manufacturing techniques will be covered, including a complete description of how you can start your own cable plant. The course will conclude with a thorough exploration of the profit potential of cable with special emphasis on overseas markets, satellites and nuclear energy plants.

#73964—AFRICA NEEDS LEADERS
(Tues., 7:30, $20)
Maurice Wakamba

Educated people are still scarce in the Third World, especially in government. If you've got a high school diploma or its equivalent, you could qualify as a Lifetime President, Prime Minister or at least a high ranking cabinet member of an African country. Learn the right survival techniques for this fast-moving field, where leadership and power are yours for the taking. All you need is the know-how to manipulate the military junta while you make lucrative business deals with the rich governments who want to exploit your country. You'll get a thorough grounding in Swiss Bank Depositing, money laundering and how to escape from a coup.

#96217—START YOUR OWN ASKING SERVICE
(Mon., 9:00, $15)
Myron Spittsbard

A burgeoning new career field is opening for professional askers. In today's fast-moving, highly specialized world there are many people who do not have the time nor the inclination to ask a lot of questions, to "pump" people for necessary information, to obtain important facts and figures through painstaking and persistent queries. Instead, they are rapidly becoming more dependent on specialists, highly trained professionals, who are experts in the area of asking—and they are ready to pay substantial fees for this essential service.

You will learn how to ask questions in every important format—telephonically, person to person and in written form. You will learn how to create questionnaires, conduct business interviews and even ask deeply personal questions for your clients. You will master every style of asking—the direct method, the tactful, diplomatic style, the scientific method, the "breezy" style. Not only will you master the art and science of asking, but you will learn how to absorb and transmit the answers effectively to your clients and record the answers on tape cassettes, which can be played back in the same manner as a telephone answering machine. As a term project you will create your own asking service and submit a five-minute tape for examination and grading.

#27534—START YOUR OWN COTTAGE INDUSTRY
(Thurs., 9:00, $50)
Maury Waftel

The answer to today's acute housing shortages may be the old-fashioned cottage. Smaller than a house, larger than a bungalow, the cottage is an ideal shelter solution for many of today's singles and young couples. In effect, it is the equivalent of a one-bedroom apartment. Maury Waftel, President of ACI, American Cottage Industries, will discuss how you can obtain an ACI franchise and sell their cottages. Or, if you wish, you can start your own cottage industry (but Waftel warns all students that he is a vicious business-

OVER-EXTENSION UNIVERSITY BULLETIN

man, a cutthroat operator who will stop at nothing to ruin his competition. Most prospective businessmen prefer to learn with ACI and buy into one of their franchises).

ACI offers three basic cottage styles, all prefabricated and delivered to the buyer as a complete design package. There is "English Country," with a plasticized thatched roof ("Lasts longer than real thatch," says Waftel); "High Tech," the modern stainless steel cottage and "African Queen," the traditional jungle style, best suited for the Sun Belt and semitropical climates.

Cottages are cute, snug and homey. Like a car, they can be ordered with dozens of options—extra rooms, appliances, wallpaper, deluxe bathrooms, etc. Waftel's staff trains you in the basics of cottage construction, then helps you set up your sales and marketing organization. Though ACI is still a suburb-oriented company, it plans to expand to the cities, despite expensive land costs, with its new "vertical concept," cottages that will be stacked in six- and twelve-story cottage complexes, complete with an elevator.

Related Courses in Careers

How to Become a Consultant on any Subject, #47382
Tax and Bomb Shelters, a Seminar, #59661
Career Opportunities in Furniture Shampooing, #17698
Speedwriting a Best-Selling Book, #05231
Small Scale Embezzling, #16324
Dance Uniform Maintenance, #46819
How to Overcome Loneliness at the Top, #19321
How to Make a Million Dollars While You Sleep, #11105
How to Break into Coal Mining, #81973
Expresso Machine Repair: Career of the 80s, #80216
How to be a "Voice Under" for TV commercials, #28436

Careers 11

OVER-EXTENSION UNIVERSITY BULLETIN

PERSONAL GROWTH

#98325–RAISING YOUR CRIMINALLY GIFTED CHILD
(Tues., 9:00, $30)
Carmine Casalaqua, Nunzio Squiglianti

Though society accepts the idea that some children are born a bit bad, we are still slow to realize that many other children are born unequivocally and brilliantly bad. These are the precocious, criminally gifted children from all walks of life who for the most part, are not encouraged and taught to develop their natural superiorities in this area. Instead, their talents go to waste, and their natural tendency to walk the tightrope between the netherworld and the mainstream of society manifests itself either in petty crimes or a lifetime career in military service.

This course offers a complete workshop for both parents and their criminally gifted children. The first session will feature the recently developed "Criminality Quotient Exam," which tests the ability of a child to make fundamental criminal distinctions. (Sample questions: Is it better to mug a bag lady or a banker? How can you tell if your father counts his change at the end of the day? Why is it more likely that a kid who is new to your school will pay you more extortion money than an older student?)

Parents will learn how to cultivate a sense of risk and danger in their child, how to judge a school on the basis of dark hallways and open playgrounds, and what career opportunities will be opening for the maturing criminal.

OVER-EXTENSION UNIVERSITY BULLETIN

#33694—WINNING THROUGH STUTTERING
Use Your Handicap and Intimidate People
(Wed., 5:30, $40)
Maria Tedesco

If you speak with a heavy stutter you have no reason to be ashamed or feel inferior. You actually possess a formidable weapon that can be used to intimidate and influence people to your point of view. It can become your strongest negotiating point. Many famous, successful people were stutterers, including Wilbur Mills, Jimi Hendrix, Lord Mountbatten and Mickey Mantle.

As a stutterer you will automatically establish sympathy for your plight. Many people will underestimate your intelligence and perhaps think you are an idiot, which will give you a distinct negotiating advantage. They will have to strain to listen to you, which will tire them and weaken their resistance to your arguments.

Maria Tedesco, a brilliant stutterer and millionairess, shows you how to use your stutter effectively. You'll learn the "Key Word" ploy—an important basic technique where you speak perfect sentences until you get to the "key word," then pretend to have terrible difficulty getting the word out. As everyone waits in agony and sympathizes with your struggle you will have them agreeing to anything you say, as long as you can finally complete your sentence. Of course, the trick is never to let them supply the key word for you. If they are exasperated and beat you to it, you have to change the word.

There will also be thorough coverage of the staccato, machine gun style of stuttering and the sickening stutter, which could cause people to make an unconsciously tasteless remark and in turn, make them feel so guilty and apologetic that they are completely at your mercy.

#11325—WINNING THROUGH OBFUSCATION
The "V" Theory of Norman Tremble
(Fri., 9:00, $20)
Ted Brownrose

While much has been made of "winning through intimidation" and other ultra-aggressive theories, a new discipline of negotiation and self-improvement is proving even more effective—the "V" Theory of Norman Tremble. "V" stands for vagueness—vagueness in all your thinking, your negotiations, your presentations, your total working style. The course is based on Mr. Tremble's best-selling book, *Six of One, Half a Dozen of the Other: The "V" Theory of Negotiation*.

Ted Brownrose, a close associate of Mr. Tremble, will teach the Tremble Method. You will learn how to keep your adversaries off balance with perfect equivocation, how to "cloud men's minds" with a mesmerizing blend of real words and double-talk. ("If we opt for the down side, we *may* have to pre-empt the krole"—note the emphasis on the word "may" and the word "krole," a nonsense word that sounds as if it has real meaning.)

You'll learn the art of creative stalling, tactics of retreat, how to win an important battle without ever making a decision, how to look intelligent without ever saying a word and how to say nothing with complete sincerity and conviction.

The classes will put you directly into practical applications of the "V" Theory, where you will negotiate against your classmates, with coaching by Mr. Brownrose.

#69782—CREATIVE NAIL BITING
(Thurs., 7:30, $20)
Bernice Groober

Conventional wisdom has always painted the picture of the nail biter as a nervous, anxiety-filled person who sublimates his neuroses into an oral fixation on his nails. Bernice Groober, author of *How to Save Thousands a Year with Teeth Manicures*, puts nail biting into an entirely new light, channeling the oral fixation into a creative, practical way to give yourself a perfect manicure. In a series of enlightening lectures, accompanied by superb slide pictures and diagrams, she shows how to trim nails perfectly, how to shape cuticles, even how to buff your nails with your tongue. Once and for all, the nail biting stigma can be eliminated and remade into a creative and constructive pastime.

#21422—MENOPAUSE AT 21: A NEW WAY TO COPE WITH STRESS
(Wed., 7:30, $15)
Jack Knorfman

There is no doubt that the stress and demands of life today require an enormous amount of mental and physical energy. The world is incredibly overpopulated. To achieve any form of success is

Personal Growth 13

growing more difficult by the day because there is very little room at the top. In fact, there is scarcely any room left in the middle. Competition for any kind of worthwhile position is becoming overwhelmingly intense. The economy grows worse. Every form of pollution increases. Education may soon become a luxury only for the super-rich. And if we think for just a moment of the lower, disadvantaged classes, we realize that their lives are so hopeless that it would take a person of super-human powers to succeed.

Jack Knorfman's solution to this problem is to "quit while you're young." He proposes that people who feel under-qualified to cope with the stress of life, who face their Success Potential with fear and trembling, who have difficulty "connecting," who lack sexual potency, who do not have the relentless drive to compete and "hustle" their way to success, should begin their menopause at age twenty-one. Instead of killing themselves slowly by refusing to recognize their inability to cope with life, they should embrace a "Change of Life" and grow old gracefully at a much earlier age.

According to Mr. Knorfman, real menopause begins on the first morning you wake up and realize you do not want to start your day, but would rather stay in bed. The mistake most young people make is getting up from their bed when their natural instincts tell them how hopeless it would be to expend their energies in a losing cause—their own lives.

Instead of wasting time trying to beat the overwhelming odds of achieving success, of getting high marks, of *winning*, Knorfman proposes a creative approach to early retirement, a carefully phased plan that will bring you into menopause in your early twenties so that you will never have to face the problems you were never equipped to handle in the first place.

The course is given in three sections: Early Withdrawal, Mastering the Techniques of Menopause, and How to Enter Your Golden Retirement Age.

Early Withdrawal is primarily a psychological orientation—an examination of your motives, your feelings and needs about going into early menopause. The second part will deal with the "hows"—how to turn, channel and sublimate your energies into positive inertia, how to withdraw from active normal life into a life of nonachievement, how to adopt the lifestyle of a senior citizen. The third section deals with how to truly enjoy your "golden years," which could be anywhere from twenty-one to ninety.

You will also study the pros and cons of the new Early Menopause Retirement Villages, how to collect social security benefits while still in your twenties, how to advance your age with safe, effective hormone treatments and the Brazilian plastic surgery technique of premature aging.

For those who can already see a future full of struggle and trauma, this new approach to life may be the one exciting and fulfilling solution.

**#98005—BROTHERS OF FAMOUS PSYCHIATRISTS
The Lesser Known But Equally Provocative Theories of George Freud, Seymour Jung and Barney Adler**
(Wed., 9:00, $20)
Paul Zugsmith

The Revisionists in psychiatry are revising their theories once again to accommodate the brilliant insights of the Freud, Jung and Adler Brothers, who were overshadowed by their more-publicized siblings.

George Freud, younger brother of Sigmund, based his findings on the influence of parental hygiene habits. Seymour Jung was preoccupied with weather cycles during a person's adolescence. Barney Adler, who was actually a dentist, was more concerned with the traumas of teething. Together, the brothers formed their own medical building in Zurich where they broke new ground in their respective fields.

#17268—HOW TO COMMUNICATE WITH YOURSELF
(Mon., 9:00, $25)
Wendy Bibbeling

One of the primary causes of neurotic behavior patterns, alienation and depression is the inability to communicate with yourself. Great emphasis has been placed on communication and connecting with others, but far too often the most important person in your life has been neglected. This course will demonstrate various practical and imaginative ways to make yourself feel loved and esteemed.

The first part of the course deals with the most direct approach—how to talk to yourself so that you can begin a relationship—how to "break the ice" and penetrate your resistance and defense mechanisms (you'd be surprised at how effective the line "Do you come here often?" is as an opener).

You will discover that the more you can open up to yourself, the deeper and more profound your relationship will be, because only *you* can respond so sensitively to your own feelers.

You'll learn how to communicate your deepest dreams and fears, your hopes and aspirations, your likes and dislikes. The more you communicate the more you will lose your inhibitions about talking to yourself. Soon you'll be talking to yourself in the mirror, making dates with yourself for dinner, drinks and movies. As Wendy

● REMEMBER: YOU CAN REGISTER FOR ANY COURSE, ANY TIME. IF YOU REGISTER IN THE MIDDLE OF A COURSE, TAKE IT AGAIN THROUGH THE PART YOU MISSED ●

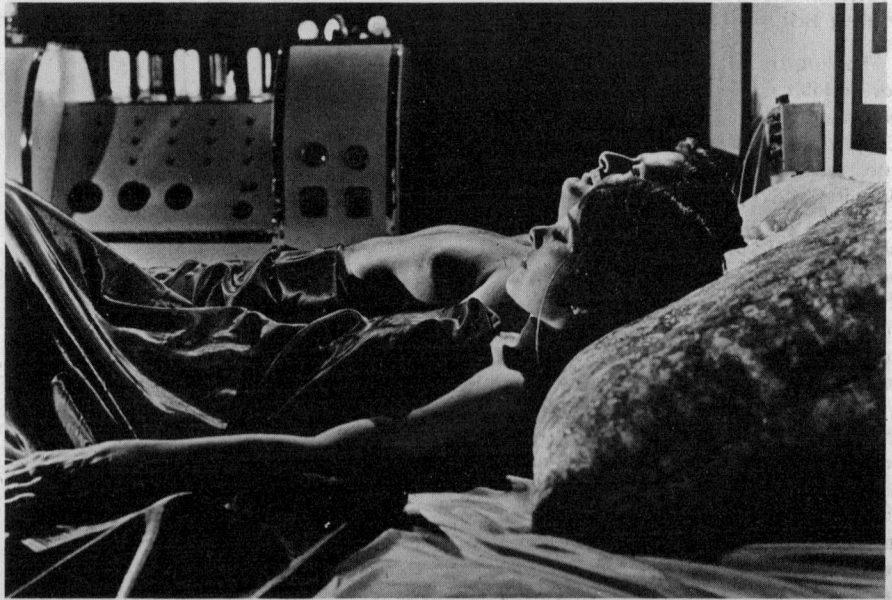

Bibbeling will constantly point out, "If you can't talk to yourself, who can you talk too?"

Of course, greater communication carries the responsibility of more effective *listening*. You'll learn the important body language of talking with yourself—how to establish eye contact, using touch to its best advantage and how to communicate disapproval without offending yourself.

The next technique you will learn is how to continue your relationship in public. You will learn how to overcome your shyness by whispering to yourself, or speaking softly into your shoulder and armpit. Once you can communicate with yourself in a normal conversational voice in public you are ready to intensify your relationship to even deeper areas of understanding. Soon you can take yourself anywhere and handle it with ease and aplomb.

The second part of the course will show you how to maintain your communication at a high level of interest, how to avoid boredom, how to create more spontaneity with yourself. You'll learn how to call yourself on the phone, how to write yourself complimentary letters and how to send yourself telegrams and gifts on special occasions (there's nothing more exciting than receiving surprises in the mail).

Other areas that will be covered are how to place personal messages in newspaper classified ad sections, how to write complimentary grafitti to yourself and how to send yourself exhilarating sky-writing messages.

#82635—ADVANCING MEDIOCRITY: THE PRE-MIDLIFE CRISIS
(Thurs., 9:00, $20)
Helen Bogash

Passing through the midlife crisis before midlife is *not* the mark of the over-achiever. Rather, suffering the Midlife Crisis before midlife is the result of the latest social phenomenon: Advancing Mediocrity. Millions of people currently suffer A.M., although they are completely unaware of it. Helen Bogash shows you how to detect the A.M. Midlife Crisis, how to pass through it while you are still young, and what to do to kill time while your friends go through the Midlife Crisis in their *actual* midlives.

Ms. Bogash contends that most men in the twenties and thirties, who have achieved a moderate degree of success yet have little promise of advancement in their economic position, (usually occupying positions in lower management or upper government) are the "New Mediocrities." As their positions become more secure and their work more routine and predictable, they become centered around new interests, such as hobbies and leisure activities. "They are more concerned with barbecue chips than silicon chips," says Ms. Bogash. "By the time they are forty, their ambition dries out, and they're ready for the great labor bonfire."

In Part I of the course, Ms. Bogash will discuss the twenty-one symptoms of A.M. Among these are:

Eager anticipation of the Little League season, especially in the single man.
The ability to discuss the merits of the Weber Barbecue Grill for more than thirty minutes.
Wearing novelty aprons, with slogans like "Do You Smell Smoke?" at the office coffee break.
A profound distaste for calendars that lump both days of the weekend into one square.

Part II of this course will center on the Post-Mid-life Crisis, and will be given next semester. Ms. Bogash is currently in the planning stages of Parts III and IV of the A.M. series: the Pre-Senility Workshop and the Pre-Death Years. In both of these, Ms. Bogash will be assisted by Nathan Albumen, the originator of the Death Bed Crisis Hotline.

● **EARN A MASTER'S DEGREE FROM OVER-EXTENSION U.** ●

Just take any twelve courses and it's yours. Our Masters Degree is printed on parchment-style paper suitable for framing, with handsome decorative borders and a fully accredited official acknowledgment of your achievement.

Twelve courses, a regular $400 value
Only $299.95
For a PHD, take any 20 courses, receive a
similar document, mounted in its own custom frame.
20 courses, a regular $600 value
Only $399.95

Related Courses in Personal Growth

Shoddy Workmanship: How to Achieve it, #01632
Weekend Seminar: Solving the Problems of the "Emotional Cripple," #02448
How to Misplace Important Items, #03672
Eye Contact: 100 Ways to Achieve It, #04896
Beauty Secrets for Your Ugly Children, #05112
How to Start Your Own Small Scale War, #06112
How to Write a Successful Shopping List, #07142
New Ways to Look at Death, #17930
How to Make Love to Yourself, #18642
Special Problems of Big-Breasted Women, #46821
Stress: How to Achieve It, #17351
Getting in Touch with Your Soul, #53172
How to Make Love to a Dolphin, #14698
Fasting in the Nude, #89641
Karma vs. Karma: How to Find Out if Your Dog Was Once King of Spain, #00135
How to Regress Into Childhood and Never Come Back, #00003
Biorythmic Breathing, #31582
Fooling Around with Your Hormones, #19947
How to Develop Your Psychic Skill with Nothing but Small Household Appliances, #19996
How to Satisfy a Nymphomaniac, #96321
Life Simplification: How to Decrease Your Vocabulary, #17814
Terminal Sex: Meeting New Lovers at Airline, Bus and Train Terminals, #51124
How to Look Intelligent Even If You're Not, #86135
Suing People for Fun and Profit, #57111
How to Toilet Train Your Dog Through Biofeedback, #23691
Ambience Chasing: How to Sneak Into Beautiful Homes and Get Decorating Ideas for Nothing, #54160
Aerobic Cooking and Real Estate Management, #06145
Winning Through Losing, #42399
How to Talk to Your Food, #79532

HEALTH

#97621–OVEREATING: THE OVERACHIEVERS DISEASE
(Fri., 9:00, $35)
Gordon Bibbeling

According to many psychiatrists and career counselors, people overeat to prove to themselves and the world that they can excel and beat others, that they must overachieve even in this basic activity. "Genuine overachievers have to be the best at everything, even eating," said Meyer Langfelder, professor of psycho-gastronomy at Stanford University, where the pioneering studies of this syndrome have been conducted.

It is the theory of Professor Langfelder that a large group of overachievers are oral-oriented, that the same urge to devour the competition in their work operates in their overwhelming desire to devour food. Food becomes a competitive rival that must be destroyed, eliminated, or more literally, "eaten." This compulsion to beat and destroy the opposition simply cannot be controlled and for many, eating is the only outlet.

After a thorough study of this problem, Mr. Bibbeling will discuss the various cures that have been developed. Some overeaters can be cured by simply chomping on pictures of their favorite foods that have been artifically flavored. Others need more drastic treatment. One school favors cryogenics, the science of freezing a person while he is still alive in the hope that when he is thawed out years later, the craving for food will be abated. Another idea is to put poisonous snakes in an overeater's refrigerator. The most effective and also the most difficult solution is to eat the nonessential parts of your own body.

#64213–QUACK MEDICINE: WHAT HAVE YOU GOT TO LOSE?
(Thurs., 9:00, $25)
Hyman Klau

Quack medicine is the last real hope for many people suffering from the so-called incurable ills. For years this area of science has suffered from ridicule and scorn, because of a few unscrupulous practitioners. In actual fact, most of the physicians working in this field are sincere, hard-working healers who must take extreme risks and venture outside the normal realm of medicine to achieve their goals. More often they succeed where their legitimate medical colleagues fail.

Hyman Klau, author of the recent *Why a Quack?, A History of Para-Normal Medicine,* will offer an historical survey of this field, dealing with the great quacks of the past and present. Each session will also feature a guest expert who will discuss and demonstrate his specialty, many of which can be applied to cure your own ills. Some of the guests will include:

Dr. Boris Rivka, a biochemist who specializes in pencil shavings research. Dr. Rivka has discovered that the ordinary shavings from pencil sharpeners can be electronically bombarded with certain chemicals and injected directly into the bloodstream where they bond themselves to the blood cells that may be responsible for certain forms of cancer. In the bonding process the cancerous cells are destroyed, never to be seen again.

You will participate in a demonstration of the controversial Duck Meat Theory of Dr. Lothar Balme, where slices of cooked duck breasts are applied to a tumor, causing the infected area to shrink and disappear.

You'll visit the laboratory of Dr. Uric Nomad, a pioneer in Saliva Therapy for hormonal imbalances and inner ear disturbances.

Dr. Irma Denoobian will demonstrate her Potted Plant technique for curing baldness.

Many other new discoveries will be covered in film and slide presentations. A special discount on all medical services will be available to the students and their immediate families.

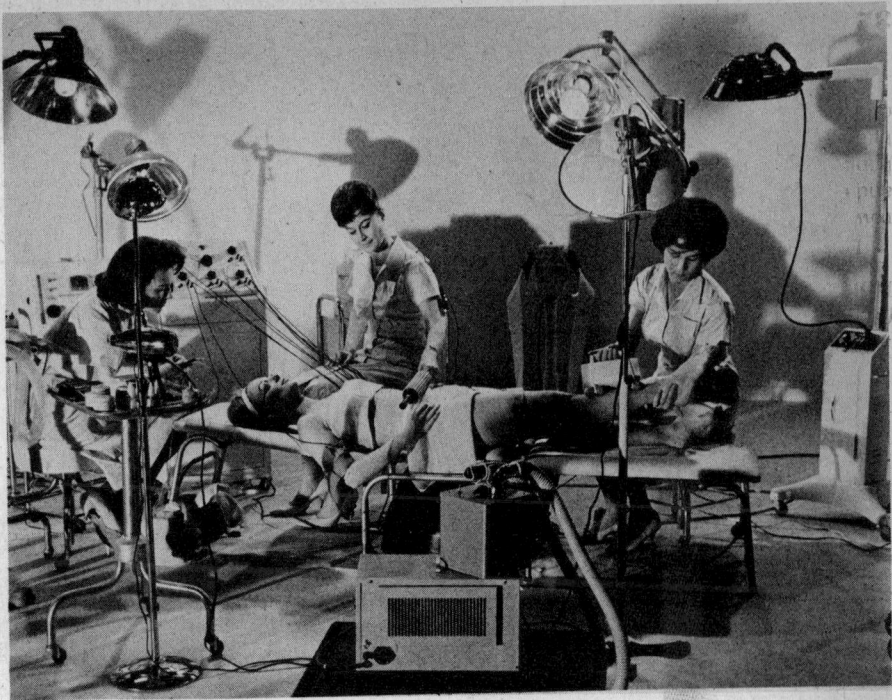

If you suffer from an annoying illness or an incurable disease, you owe it to yourself to explore a course that could end up saving your life or the life of a loved one. As Dr. Rivka once said, "With an incurable disease, what have you got to lose?"

● ALL SENIOR CITIZENS QUALIFY FOR HALF-PRICE DISCOUNTS ON SELECTED COURSES GIVEN AFTER 11:15 PM. ●

See Mal or Tony for details. room 417.

FOR SENIOR CITIZENS

#65354—HOW TO ENJOY REGULAR BOWEL MOVEMENTS
(Wed., 3:30, $15)
Ross Schingleburger

One of the chronic problems of growing older is the loss of "regularity," a touchy, sensitive subject that is either handled with kid gloves or becomes the tasteless joke of mediocre comedians. This course approaches the problem straightforwardly and realistically, without euphemisms and apologies, recognizing the fact that waste elimination is a daily fact of life, presenting a severe problem to the senior citizen. The goal of the course is to reinstate regularity to its rightful position—as the center of thoughtful, intelligent conversation.

Ross Schingleburger, who is ninety-six years old, is a specialist in this area, and the developer of a natural method of attaining regularity called Colonic Dancing. Similar to Aerobic Dancing, but not as strenuous, it involves the exercise of that area of the mid-section, where the colon is located. The movements are done to the

rhythms of rock 'n' roll and disco music. The idea of Colonic Dancing is to "shake, rattle and roll" your colon until it becomes a finely tuned, flexible, efficient organ. Dr. Schingleburger eschews laxatives and drugs of all kinds, even the so-called "natural" ones. He believes in rejuvenating this tired, pampered organ by exercise alone. Your colon *can* be pushed and coaxed into its "second youth," just as the heart muscle can be strengthened, without the use of harsh and dangerous stimulants. The final session features a special awards dinner, at which successful dancers receive bronzed chilidogs.

#22468–OVERCOMING HYPNOSIS THROUGH FEAR
(Tues., 7:30, $25)
Professor Henry Stiff

Hypnosis as a form of medical treatment is fast becoming a drug-like habit, a fraudulent panacea for life's ills that is actually causing more harm than good. When administered by a professional, hypnosis can become a deadly form of mind control, transforming the patient into a malleable zombie, a robot with no mind of his own. Even when self-administered, hypnosis can eventually cause brain damage and bizarre behavior.

This course will teach you how to resist all forms of hypnosis, meditation and the so-called "relaxation therapies" through the tried and true method of *Mind Cluttering*. You will also learn easy, foolproof ways to resist hypnosis by creating extra fear, tension, anxiety and hysteria within yourself as defense mechanisms. The concluding sessions will concentrate on exercises for obtaining optimum muscle rigidity.

#75239–BODY ODOR LANGUAGE
How to Interpret Body Odor as a Semiotic Concept of Our Times
(Tues., 9:00, $20)
Christopher Kringle

Although there have been many studies of Body Language and Movement, the research into body odors is still in the pioneering stage. Yet it is possible that this area will yield even greater insights than body language in the exploration of man's behavior in the modern world.

Mr. Kringle will discuss the seven basic Body Odor Types: All-Meat and Alcohol; Chicken, Veal, Fish and Vegetable; Chicken, Fish and Vegetable; Fish and Vegetable; All-Vegetable; All-Grain; and the Mystic.

He will show you how to detect the various odors and how odors are influenced by the media, sports, fashions and architecture. Mr. Kringle will assist you in creating your own Body Odor Profile. This unique profile will help you to understand how you and your odors relate to your culture and environment and how you can improve and enhance your lifestyle.

#34768–THE SMOKE DETECTOR'S DIET
How to Lose Weight Through Smoking
(Thurs., 7:30, $25)
Shelly Bogash, Executive Director, Smoke Detectors, Unlimited

The Smoke Detector's Diet is based on the simple principle that people who smoke heavily require less food. Their appetites are usually dulled and their taste buds are more desensitized than nonsmokers. Therefore, the more weight you want to lose the more cigarettes you must smoke. As you build your intake of tobacco you will discover that you need surprisingly little food. The result is a dramatic loss of excess weight that will transform you into a more youthful-looking, vibrant person, with a lean, taut body that is so perfect for today's chic fashions. Classes will cover every facet of the Diet including how to choose the correct brand of tobacco, how to inhale properly and special lung and throat toughening exercises. The program breaks you in with "real tobacco" cigarettes such as Camels, Luckies, Gauloise and other powerful foreign brands. Low-tar low-nicotine filter brands that could increase your appetite are never used. You should begin to see results by the end of the first day!

Depending upon the individual's tobacco tolerances, the program tries to get you up to at least six packs a day within a week. The actual diet could consist of "Beans 'n' Butts," "Steak 'n' Smokes," "Fish 'n' Fags" or the Crash Programs—the Cigarettes and Whiskey Diet and the special Cigarettes and Coffee Diet.

Note: A large selection of stylish smoking jackets and pants, in many colors and fabrics, perfect training apparel for the Smoke Detector's Diet, are available at the school clothing boutique in the north lobby.

#75693–A HISTORY OF SHAVING & SHAVING TECHNIQUES WORKSHOP
(Wed., 9:00, $20)
Seymour Kreml

The course will be given in two parts: an historical survey of shaving, followed by the Shaving Techniques Workshop.

The art and science of shaving is a truly fascinating subject that offers startling new insights into the cultural patterns of civilizations from ancient times to the present. Mr. Kreml will analyze the shaving customs of many peoples from a psycho-biographical, Marxist and socio-cultural point of view to form a firmly balanced perspective.

The Egyptians shaved their faces with trained locusts and a species of termite that would eat away at their beards. Most of these highly skilled insects were trained by the royal barbers and were available only to the privileged classes. The Alexandria Rebellion instigated the first acts of shaving legislation in history.

The Alexandria Rebellion of 1218 B.C. was not a politically inspired act, but was actually caused by acute shaving material shortages among the lower classes. After petitioning the local chiefs, the priests and the Pharoah himself to no avail, a group of rebels under the leadership of Tuk Ra seized control of Alexandria's main storehouse of shaving materials and distributed them to the people.

Shaving techniques remained primitive for many centuries. The Greeks used small pecking birds. The Japanese endured hot stones that burned away their beards. In the Middle Ages, the blood-sucking leech was also used for facial hair. And in Central Europe and the Baltic States, the people plucked out their hairs one by one with a crude wooden version of a tweezer.

Mr. Kreml will discuss many other unusual shaving techniques including Chinese firecrackers and South American piranhas. He will conclude with the modern era, which begins with the use of jagged glass and the knife, and finally, the razor. With the invention of shaving soap in 1706 by Geoffrey Soap of Brighton, England, shaving became a genuinely refined form, a precursor of today's highly sophisticated techniques.

The Shaving Workshop is a course that will show you how to achieve the state of the art in shaving yourself. Various techniques will be discussed—single and double applications, the pros and cons of different creams and blades, the role of the electric shaver and how to work with the "problem faces," such as "five o'clock shadow" and extra-sensitive skin.

There will be demonstrations of the shaving art by professional barbers and

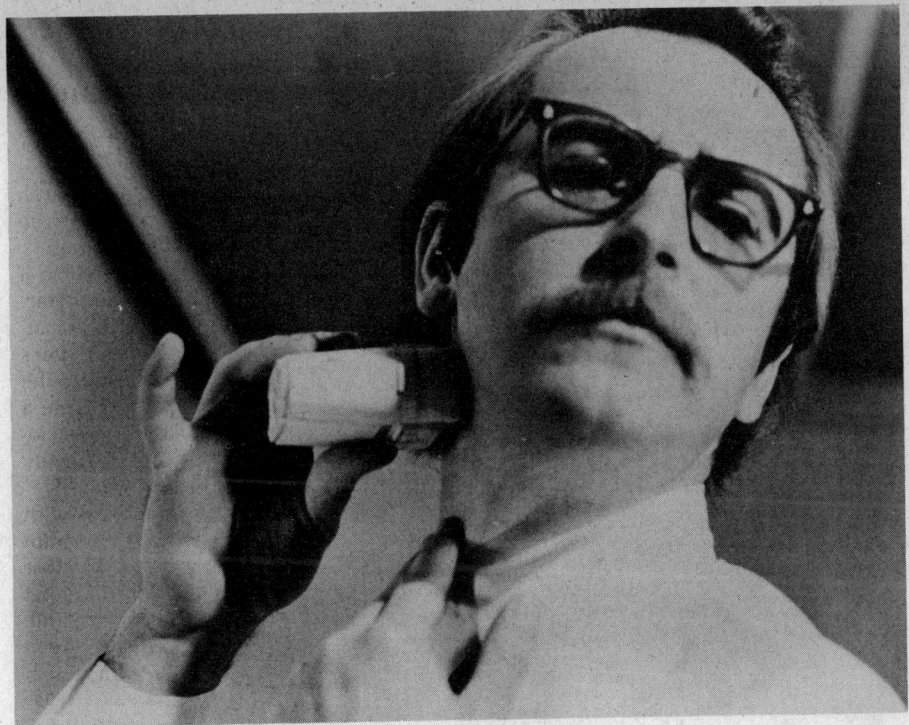

each student will be asked to shave himself in order to get a complete shaving analysis and profile (your shaving rights and wrongs) by the professionals.

In conclusion, Mr. Kreml will show a film produced by the Gillette Safety Razor Company called *Shaving: 2001*, a remarkable depiction of what shaving will be like in the 21st century. You'll see exciting new products that are still on the drawing board and some which are only a few years away, including the razorless shave, and a new aerosol spray that seeps into your pores with its special enzymes and extracts your facial hairs. You'll also see the newest ideas in shavers such as the sonic wave and laser beam models. A representative from the Gillette Company will be on hand to answer your questions and demonstrate some of the more advanced products.

#98426–TIBETAN NOSTRIL MASSAGE
(Wed., 9:00, $15)
Tanya Beck

One of the tragic consequences of becoming an adult in western society is the blind adherence to certain taboos you were smart enough to ignore when you were a child. A perfect example is nostril massage. For years this practice has been ignored, ridiculed and outrightly prohibited in polite society. It is only within the last two or three years that this perfectly natural activity has come to be recognized by medical authorities to carry enormous, life-enhancing benefits.

Tanya Beck, a physical therapist and anthropologist has led many expeditions to Tibet, Nepal and Russia where she has worked with the primitive, "uncivilized" mountain tribes who still practice this ancient technique. She has discovered that the average lifespan of those tribesmen practicing nostril massage is 109 years, and many live to be 150 and more!

Nostril massage is an integral part of the life of these peoples, as natural as eating, sleeping and making shoes with curled-up toes. Throughout their waking (and even sleeping) hours they would always have at least one finger in their nostrils doing some kind of light or heavy massage.

"There seems to be no doubt that nostril massage is of immense value to the circulatory system," said Ms. Beck. "It develops good nostril muscle tone, cleanses the system to help you breathe better and we are pretty sure it prevents hardening of the arteries, hence giving you a longer life."

Ms. Beck teaches the Tibetan technique which massages both nostrils simultaneously, using the index finger alternating with the pinky. Although this is by far the most difficult technique to master, it is well worth it for efficiency and longevity. Ms. Beck will also teach some of the simpler methods including the Russian "All-Thumbs" and the Nepalese "Butterfly" stroke. Tissues and washing facilities will be provided.

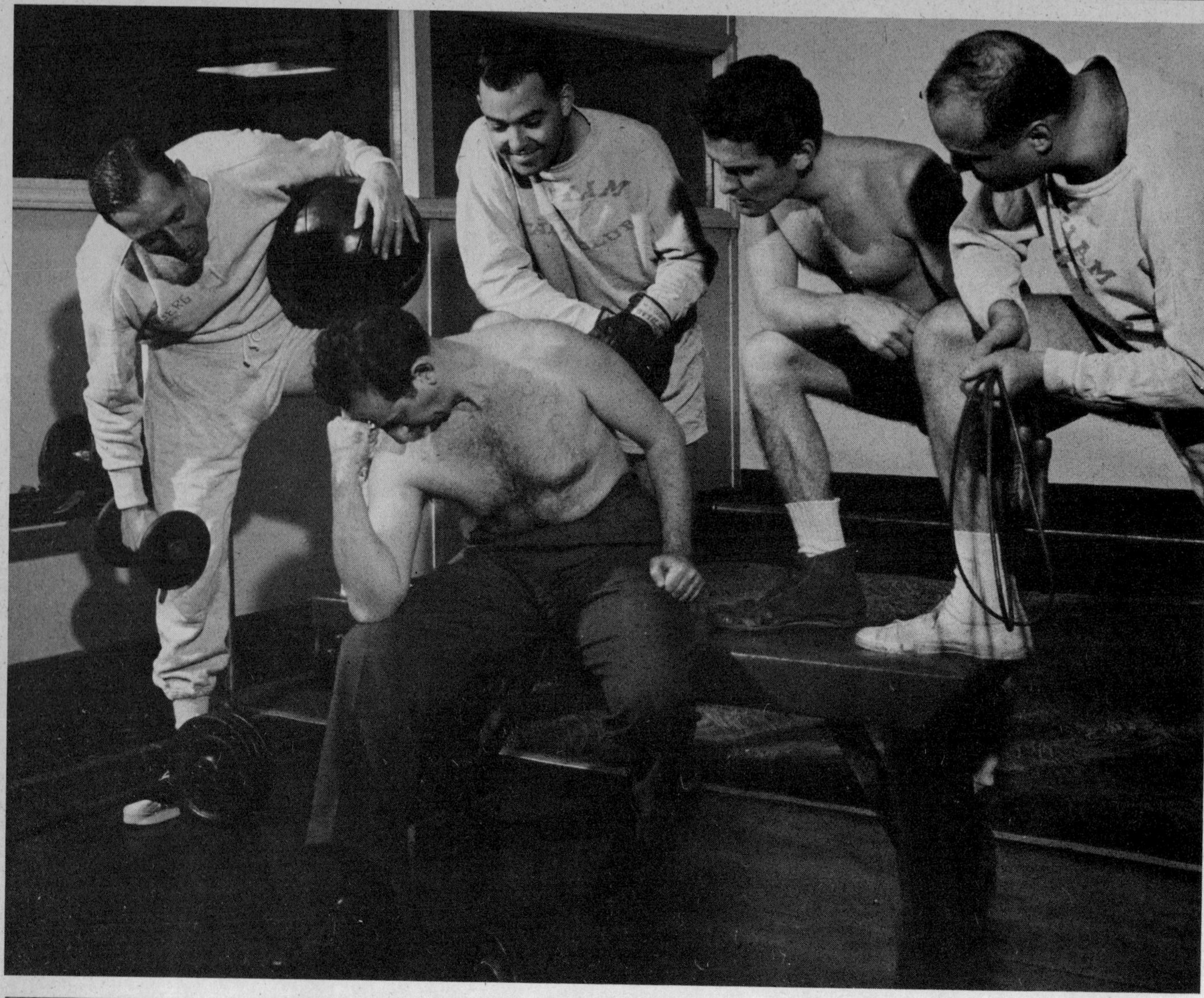

PHYSICAL FITNESS

#68249–H'AI L'AI
The Japanese Art of Trembling and Fear
(Tues., 7:30, $25)
Ichiko Tarasawa

H'ai L'ai is a Japanese martial art even older than the conventional forms, recognizing the mind-shattering power you can unleash through self-humiliation. Ichiko Tarasawa is a Black Hanky in H'ai L'ai and is the protégé of Toko Yosenabe, the famous "Mad Groveler of Kyoto." He will teach you basic crying, whimpering and moaning techniques; how to beg for mercy and how to develop a piercing scream.

The second part of the course will concentrate on groveling techniques—how to humble and debase yourself, licking shoes, socks, calves (if your attacker is wearing anklets) and so on, right up to wet kisses. The final phase of the course deals with special emergency techniques such as willing an epileptic fit on yourself, and creating various forms of palsy and Parkinson's Disease.

#36222–SONY
The New Japanese Art of Self-Defense
(Mon., 9:00, $20)
Yakamoko Kon

A new, easy-to-learn martial arts discipline has emerged from Japan called *Sony*, the art of self-defense using battery-operated small appliances, gadgets and stereo equipment. (*Sony* is pronounced "So-neeeeee," in a prolonged scream, as you use your small appliance to destroy an attacker.)

Yakamoko Kon, a mauve belt in *Sony* will teach you the art of throwing small TV sets, radios, travel clocks and pencil sharpeners at your assailants, causing permanent injury, and if you wish, instant death. You'll learn how to strangle an attacker with your Sony Walkman headset, how to strike, swipe and swing your equipment, turning a potential mugger or rapist into a brain-damaged vegetable.

Mr. Kon also teaches other martial arts disciplines that have been spawned out of *Sony* such as *Toshiba* (the scream is pronounced "To-sheeeeeba"), the art of using the "big black box," the all in one radio-TV-cassette player as a blunt instrument of death. For advanced students there is *Yamaha* (pronounced "Ya-ma-ha!"), in which small motorcycles and pianos are hurled at your attacker, crushing his skull.

#99627–HOW TO HYPNOTIZE YOUR RUNNING SHOES
(Tues., 9:00, $20)
Greg Shaymus

As everyone knows, the runner's weakest link is his feet, that complex collection of bone, muscle, tissue and blood that must bear the continual pounding and shock of every running stride. A flourishing branch of medicine has developed out of the running and jogging craze, as foot injuries and odd runner's ailments multiply like weeds after a summer rain.

While acknowledging the validity of podiatric research, Greg Shaymus, a graduate student in sports-shoe medicine, feels that there is even more to learn and benefit from the running footwear itself. "If the shoe fits, it will bear most of the running burden," claims Shaymus.

"The running shoe has evolved into a 'state of the art,' highly sophisticated, scientifically designed product that can almost carry you along as if you were flying off the ground," says Shaymus. He feels that the big breakthrough in curing runner's ills will be shoe medicine, in which the shoe will have a life of its own, and can be treated like part of the foot itself.

To confirm this, Shaymus has devised a set of exercises that will enable you to hypnotize your running shoes so that they will bear virtually all the burdens that would normally affect your feet.

The exercises vary according to the distance and proficiency of the runner. Joggers who run up to three miles need only a ten minute hypnosis session. Long distance runners and marathoners need at least thirty minutes to put their shoes into a complete trance.

Mr. Shaymus will instruct you in how to create the proper relaxing mood for your shoes; how to put each part of the shoe—(toe, box, arch, inner sole, heel counter, outersole, even the laces) into a perfect state of oneness with your feet, so that the shoe literally carries you aloft and absorbs all the shocks of a long, hard run.

At the end of a run, the hypnotic trance of a shoe is broken by simply taking it off and snapping your fingers at it two or three times.

#67835–TURKISH TOWEL SNAPPING
(Thurs., 9:00, $15)
Gregor Haki

Part gymnastics, part dance and part sport, *Yevti*, or Turkish Towel Snapping is fast becoming a popular new form of physical fitness for those who are growing increasingly bored with jogging, swimming and racquetball.

Yevti can be played in pairs or with as many people as you like. The players can wear shirts or other tops but everyone must be nude from the waist down. The object of the game is to take a Turkish towel, dampen it, wring it out and twist it until it is as taut as possible, and then "snap" the towel at your opponent, trying to nail him in the genital area. He, of course, is trying to do the same thing to you. The winner is judged on a simple point system.

This is merely the basic form of *Yevti*. It becomes increasingly complex and exciting as new techniques are mastered. Gregor Haki, four-time national champion of Turkey and a Black Towel in *Yevti* will offer complete instruction in basic and advanced styles, including how to coil your towel into a deadly weapon, how to use your wrists for the proper snap, the follow-through and defense moves, various backhand and forehand snaps and many other virtuoso strokes that can rival the moves of champion fencers and the leaps and turns of ballet dancers.

All you need is your own towel, preferably a clean one because you will be attacking the bare genital area. Beginners will practice with medium-size face and hand towels. Advanced students will use full-size regulation Turkish bath towels. Mr. Haki also operates a *Yevti* Pro Shop where you can buy genital ointments, salves, powders and Moktar Turkish Towels endorsed by Mr. Haki, and used successfully in international tournament play.

Related Courses in Health and Fitness

How to Use Medieval Weapons for Self Defense, #19380

How to Use Hard Drugs in Moderation, #18364

Discojazztapstretchballet-O-Metrics, #17345

How to Flatten Your Facial Cheeks, #16321

How to Grow New Teeth When You're Over Sixty, #15304

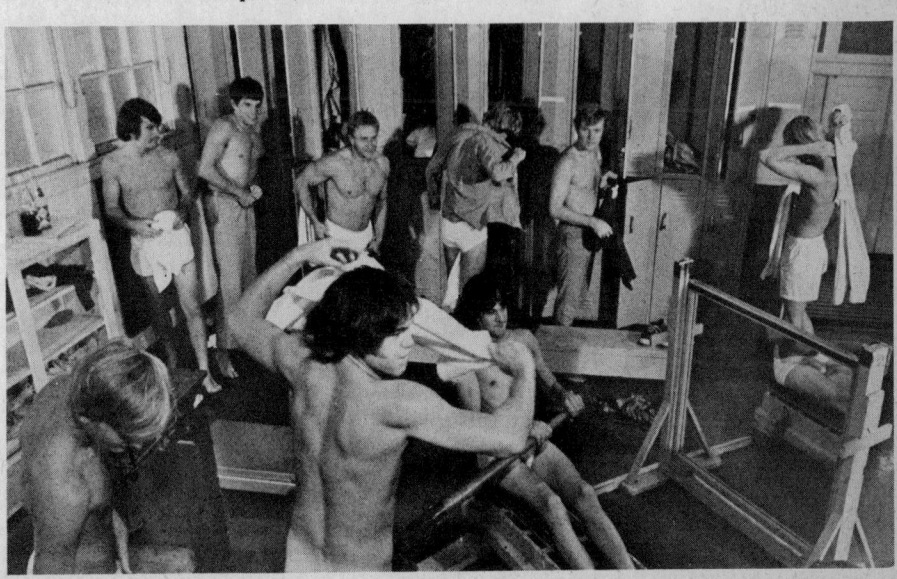

OVER-EXTENSION UNIVERSITY BULLETIN

CONSUMER AFFAIRS

#91165–DIRECT MARKETING
How to Buy Food, Clothing, Drugs, Sundries, and Other Essential Items
(Fri., 7:30, $25)
Norman Turlman

Direct marketing techniques will become increasingly important in the years to come as consumerism becomes a more significant part of our life. Every item we buy, from a toothpick to a television set must be chosen with extreme care. Mr. Turlman will discuss how to buy all the essentials of life—concentrating on food, beverages, clothing, drugs and sundries.

He will try to explain unit pricing in supermarkets, how to break the date codes of food manufacturers, how to take advantage of supermarket price wars and how to buy everything wholesale. In conclusion he will conduct an all-day shopping trip where you can buy as much as a year's supply of basic items.

● ALL MAJOR DOMESTIC AND FOREIGN CREDIT CARDS ARE ACCEPTED ●

#19382–TAKING THE MYSTERY OUT OF BUYING SALT
(Tues., 9:00, $15)
Betty Brownapple

Just as you can learn how to buy a good diamond, a fur coat or a fine piece of furniture, you can also learn how to buy good salt. Once the arcane esoterica and the myths are stripped away we will discover that salt is a simple, yet fascinating subject to learn and should not be regarded with the same fear and trepidation as differential calculus.

Betty Brownapple, formerly a consultant with the Morton Salt Company, gives you a brief history of salt, discusses how modern salt is made, how to store salt, and describes the various types and how to evaluate the kind of salt that is right for you, both in taste and nutritional value. A special salt-buying trip will be conducted with emphasis on gourmet and ethnic varieties—coarse kosher, sea salt, Chinese and the organic "natural" types. There will also be opportunities for comparison shopping and buying in bulk.

#18364–HOW TO ORDER CHINESE FOOD IN ITALIAN
(Wed., 7:30, $25)
Arthur DiBrodo

For most travelers and vacationers Italy is the favorite place to visit, for its scenic beauty, its people and the ineffable atmosphere that makes you a welcome visitor almost at once. One of the most important new developments in Italy is the sudden popularity of Chinese food everywhere. If you plan to travel to Italy for business or pleasure, this course will greatly aid you in interpeting the Chinese menu and communicating with the staff, all of whom are native Italians. Classes are intense and concentrate only on the essential phrases you need to know.

You will learn to use such phrases as "*Ancora un po, di riso, per favore*" ("Could I have more rice, please?"); "*Ci porti delle chopsticks?*" ("Could we have chopsticks?"); "*Potremmo avere della salsa d'anitra e della senape?*" ("Could we have more duck sauce and mustard?"); "*Benche non e sulla corta, avete il Pollo dal Gusto Meraviglioso?*" ("It's not on the menu, but do you have Wonderful Taste Chicken?").

Actual menus and food will be used whenever possible. Professional actors and actresses will serve as waiters and waitresses to add even more authenticity to the learning situation and help shed the "language inhibitions" you may have. For the concluding session the class will visit a Chinese restaurant in "Little Italy" and order an entire Chinese meal in Italian.

#28562–HOW TO BORROW FOOD
(Thurs., 9:00, $40)
Hilda Scrofula

Food borrowing is fast becoming an important solution to coping with today's high cost of living. Food borrowing is no longer the simple "Can you spare a cup of sugar, I'll pay you back tomorrow" idea. Today it has become a true art that can be cultivated and developed into a genuine means of sustenance for those who feel the pinch of hard times.

Hilda Scrofula, author of *Can I Borrow a Cup of Dinner for Life?*, offers a truly comprehensive approach to what may prove to be the most vital course you will ever take. First, there are the basic techniques: finding the right neighbors, friends, etc., who have unlimited generosity, ingratiating yourself, discussing food and recipes with your prospective lenders to give them the feeling that you are a good cook and a good food loan prospect. You will learn how to create your own food borrowing "image"—for example, that of a lovable but scatter-brained cook who never remembers to pay anything back.

Most important, you will become proficient at borrowing small amounts of food from large groups of people, amounts so trivial that they wouldn't dream of expecting repayment. At the same time you will be spacing your lenders carefully to avoid repetition, so that you are able to accumulate enough food to give you three meals a day, every day. Basic course includes borrowing salt, sugar, flour, spices, pasta, grains, eggs, some vegetables and fruit. The advanced course concentrates on how to borrow meat, chicken and fish. For advanced students there is also a special workshop in the art of borrowing complete main dishes such as casseroles, stews, steaks, chops and lobsters done to your order. There will also be one session devoted to the borrowing of liquor and wine.

#38192–A GUIDE TO LAWYER'S FLEA MARKETS
How to Get Fairly Adequate Legal Service at a Fraction of the Regular Costs
(Fri., 7:30, $30)
Lawrence Kugl and Tufti Halva

One of the solutions to the astronomical costs of legal services is the Lawyer's Flea Market, a new grass roots movement that is gaining support with consumer advocates all over the country. Lawyer's Flea Markets offer almost all the services of regular attorneys for far less money. The reasons? Very, very low overhead, no fancy offices, no retinue of high-priced assistants, no telephones or computers or librarians. Just plain legal advice, cash and carry.

Most of the lawyers who practice at the Flea Market are well qualified, but for one reason or another, have lost their licenses or dropped out of formal practice, so they must charge lower rates. Lawrence Kugl, a once brilliant trial lawyer who still practices at the Louis Brandeis Flea Market, provides a highly informative guide to finding the best flea market lawyer for your needs. You'll find out where to get a divorce for only $1.59, where to get a good real estate lawyer for only $3.50, and how to file a medical malpractice suit for only $5 to $17.50. Even some of the most complex corporate law cases can be handled. Many theatrical lawyers work in flea markets.

Tufti Halva, a native of Lebanon, and law student for a year in Beirut, will teach you the basics of haggling, which will be expected when you discuss fees. You will learn how to be a skillful flea bargainer—ruthless, cynical, contemptuous, diplomatic, accommodating and totally winsome as you shop for the best legal service at the lowest prices.

#99801–LEGAL RIGHTS OF DOMESTICATED, TRAINED ANIMALS
(Tues., 9:00, $25)
Bernard Jugularsky

Pet owners are facing new threats and dangers from Animal Protection Societies and other local pet do-gooders who regularly institute civil and criminal law suits against them for negligence and other forms of abuse. Mr. Jugularsky, the attorney for "Fear," Lee Marvin's German shepherd, in the country's first "Dogimony" suit, shows you how to protect yourself from unnecessary lawsuits, how to revise your will to avoid animal probate, how to buy the best animal liability, and medical life insurance and most important, how to avoid high legal fees for these crucial new services.

#114627–WHAT COLOR IS YOUR CHECKBOOK?
(Tues., 7:30, $30)
Barbara Bogash

Most people decide on the color and style of their checks and checkbook in a hurried moment at the bank. Little do they realize the importance of this decision. What color checks are right for *you*? Do you wish to convey the subdued motif, or would you rather go for the specialized "art" look? What about birds? Flowers? Wildlife? Or the new "studio" checks, which bring a lighthearted touch to one of life's more mundane activities, featuring cartoons and humorous captions such as "Don't worry, I'm not leaving town," and "My number is unlisted, but the State Pen's isn't!"

Your checkbook is one of the most important and visible ways to display your status, your financial power, and your true station in life. "Your checkbook is your window on the world," Mrs. Bogash claims. "The way you personalize your checks is your invitation to enter it. Your checks can become an asset in your life—or they can literally lead you to ruin!"

Barbara Bogash discusses the many types and styles of checkbooks and will perform an individual "Checkbook Analysis and Profile" for each class member. The last class will feature a checkbook fashion show, which will demonstrate how to color-coordinate your wardrobe with your checks to create a forceful, commanding presence in business, society and at the liquor store.

#09897—GETTING AHEAD AT THE SUPERMARKET
(Mon., 7:30, $15)
Max Zoroaster

How many times have you stood on a supermarket checkout line for what seemed like hours, wasting precious time that you could have used for more rewarding pursuits? This course teaches you the techniques and tricks (legal and slightly illegal) on how to choose the fastest-moving line, how to cheat on the 10 Items or Less Express Line, the "bump and squirm" technique of edging your cart ahead of others, the right way to ingratiate yourself ahead of others when you only have a couple of things to check out. Learn how to make your shopping trips a game of skill and bravado, and meet many attractive, bright people with the same interests and ideals as yours.

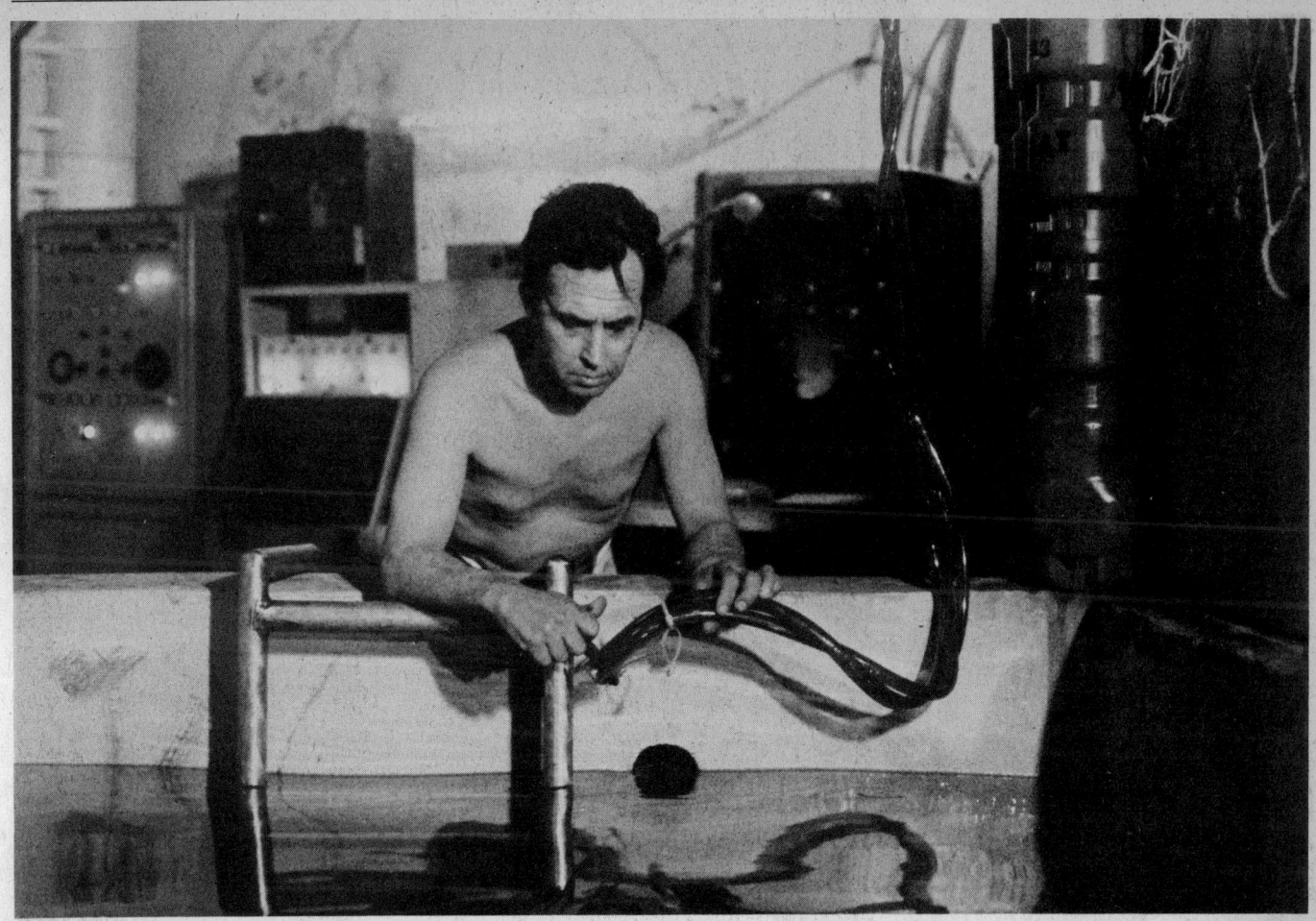

INVESTMENTS

#39476–INVESTING IN ASIAN WINE FUTURES
(Mon., 9:00, $45)
G. Murray Bumbardo

Investing in wine futures has become a complex, costly process, if one is concentrating on the more desirable European and American wines. Unless you are among the wealthy few your chances of buying anything decent are getting slimmer by the minute, either for immediate drinking or for laying down and eventual resale. G. Murray Bumbardo, an international liquor and wine drinker, explores the vast untapped potential of the new Asian wines—the wines of China, Korea, India, Tibet and Vietnam.

At the time of this writing, prices of Asian wines were still far below their French and Californian counterparts—almost ridiculously lower. For instance, a Szechuan *Kam Man* (pronounced "Gum-Man") which is roughly similar to our Californian Zinfandel except that it is colored blue, retails for $5 a case. Or a nearly drinkable Korean Riesling, which could be made more palatable with soda, lemon and lots of ice, is just $2.50 a case. (Whereas a good Alsatian Riesling costs upwards of $10.00 a bottle.)

Mr. Bumbardo takes you on an exciting wine odyssey through Asia, sampling many new vintages, discussing their characteristics, their potential, their similarities and differences to the better known wines of the western world. You'll taste the two finest wines of China, Château Wong and Yangtze Valley Late Harvest Gewurztraminer. Chateau Wong is a big, dark, Cabernet-like wine with a pungent bouquet reminiscent of clams in black bean sauce and a mysterious flavor that suggests camphor and asparagus and overtones of mustard. It is still highly tannic however, and will need at least thirty years of storage before it can be truly enjoyed. Yangtze Valley Late Harvest Gewurztraminer is a sweet dessert wine in the style of Chateau D'Yquem, the legendary Sauterne. The raw materials of this wine (which are still unknown) are cultivated and picked at the last possible moment, even beyond the "noble rot" stage, possibly in the landfill stage. The result is a wine that produces a residual sugar content of over 90 percent.

Other wines to be discussed and tasted are *Yona*, the Indian white wine made of *ghee* (clarified butter); *Dindar*, a slightly bitter grayish wine from Tibet; the bright, sparkling, nearly explosive wines of Korea and some unusual Vietnamese jug wines that are about a tenth of the price of Gallo (the Vietnamese wines should be boiled gently for thirty minutes before drinking).

Investments   **25**

#55542–HOW TO MANAGE YOUR $5 STOCK PORTFOLIO
(Wed., 7:30, $40)
Gary Dimple

Yes, there is still room for the small investor in today's volatile stock market if he knows how to pick his stocks carefully and is not afraid to take calculated risks. The object of this course is to invest no more than $5 and still create a well-rounded portfolio that promises to double, even triple your initial investment.

Gary Dimple, formerly with the Vinnie Carbonara Stock Broker Investment Company, is an expert in managing low-budget portfolios and has helped thousands of neophyte investors gain a modest toehold in the market starting with nothing but "mad money." He writes and publishes *The Dimple Line*, a weekly newsletter for the $5 investor. With Dimple as your guide, you will learn never to plunge your entire $5 into one stock or bond. The cardinal rule is: diversify—divide and conquer—play the percentages and the odds are that one or more of your stocks will make enough money to carry the rest.

Nor will Dimple allow you to invest in one *field* such as defense, retailing, utilities or computers. Instead you will be taught how to maintain a near-perfect proportion of stocks, bonds and other investments that will cover any size tremor in the market. A typical Dimple portfolio might include:

- Soft Industries (three shares at 18¢ a share)
- Mason-Dixon Lines (two shares at 12¢ a share)
- Consolidated-Block (one share at 40¢ a share)
- Gypsy Vagabond Stores (three shares at 31¢ a share)
- North American International (two shares at 28¢ a share)
- One Uganda Government Bond ($1.59)
- One dollar in mung bean futures
- Total: $4.96

This leaves a balance of 4¢ which can still be invested in a speculative stock just for the fun of it, such as Flying Hippo Airlines, Bus-Line Vending Machines or Thalidomide, Inc.

You'll study the market with one of the canniest, most colorful investors in the business, a man whose newsletter is filled with adages and truisms that have made him the most respected man in his field. Here are a few typical examples which you might want to copy and pin on your wall: "Trendy, glamour stocks are one-way tickets to nowhere"; "Specialization can lead you down the garden path right to the outhouse"; "Spread yourself thin and you'll fatten your wallet"; and the oft-quoted "I never met a stock I didn't like at one time or another."

#95768–CONVERT YOUR APARTMENT TO A CO-OP AND CONVERT TO JUDAISM
(Fri., 7:30, $45)
Solomon Klipspringer

If there ever were a pair of trends that go together it's co-op and Judaism conversion. The knowledge of city rental laws, financing an apartment building purchase, creating offering plans and other intricacies of municipal real estate seems to be the specialty of Jewish people. You'll find that once you convert to Judaism you'll convert your apartment into a profitable co-op in a much easier, trouble-free manner. Just being Jewish will give you an instinctive knowledge of the field. You'll get more respect, more access to moneymen. And you don't have to be circumcised to convert. A smart, sensible way to meet an Orthodox Jewish male.

#34980–COLLECTING ANTIQUE CHEESE
(Thurs., 9:00, $25)
Dr. Frank Nidelinger

After antique furniture, antique cars and antique clothing, what's next? According to the *Wall Street Journal* and *Forbes* magazine, it's antique cheese. Beautiful old Bries and Camemberts, Italian Country Fontinas with that dark, burnished rind, early American Monterey Jacks and Liederkranz and much more. Learn how to find, identify and collect hundreds of rare old cheeses that are growing more valuable by the day. Learn to tell the difference between a genuine antique Parmesan and a new reproduction; how to spot an old cheesemaker's trademark; how to smell the difference between a new and an antique cheese; how cheese are "faked" as antiques. You'll go on cheese antiquing tours, attend a gala cheese auction and meet other aspiring collectors—a field that is attracting thousands of single, wealthy investors.

● WE ALSO ACCEPT CHECKS, MONEY ORDERS, CASH AND STAMPS. ●

#68728–THE NEW COLLECTIBLES FOR THE 80s
Take-out Pizza Boxes, Decorative Toothpicks and More
(Fri., 9:00, $25)
Jay Speck
I. Phillip Tortone

In today's fickle, fast-moving world of changing tastes and trends what you threw in the garbage or flushed down the toilet yesterday may become tomorrow's hot new collectible. Collectibles are the "now" antiques—common, familiar items that don't appear to have any cachet until *you* start collecting them. And then watch those market values soar!

The trick is to detect which items will become truly valuable. For instance, in the area of take-out pizza boxes, anything with the slogan, "You've Tried the Rest, Now Try the Best" is worth ten times more than a pie box with the words "Hot Pizza" on it. Dry cleaning memorabilia (old receipts, plastic garment bags with ad slogans, Dry Cleaning Institute posters) is gaining great popularity. Junk mail, once considered a nuisance, is now a coveted collectible, especially mail-order pork product catalogs and anything from a lunatic religious group.

Some collectors will hoard everything, as long as it's mundane and boring, waiting to cash in on the possible backlash reaction against the more exotic collectibles. In this area, you'll find a strong interest in used Trac II shaving cartridges (not Atra), gigantic two liter plastic bottles of Diet Pepsi, brand name chicken hang tags (Perdue, Holly Farms, Paramount, Cookin' Good) and the ubiquitous decorative toothpick, the kind with the crinkly colored cellophane used on triple decker sandwiches (in a recent auction, a complete set—containing twenty-five different colors—sold for what Mr. Speck has termed "nice money").

Mr. Speck and Mr. Tortone will discuss how to gauge the investment potential of collectibles, showing you why an object may have real value; which ones possess a naive, folk-art quality; how to authenticate and appraise; how to store and insure your collectibles; and most important, when to sell them for a large fortune!

Related Course in Investments

Dust Collecting: Inexpensive Investment of the 80s, #91836

OVER-EXTENSION UNIVERSITY BULLETIN

HOBBIES

#75824–PAINTING WITH FOOD
(Mon., 7:30, $25)

#75825–ADVANCED PAINTING WITH FOOD
(Mon., 9:00, $25)
Jack Zwigman

More and more painters are turning to food as their basic working material. Today's modern convenience foods, with their generous amounts of additives and preservatives, are actually far more versatile and economical than paint. There is already enough scientific evidence to prove that a "food canvas" will last infinitely longer than any painted one. They simply cannot—and *will* not—deteriorate.

The introductory course gives you a thorough grounding in how to work with the latest foods, the aerosol sprays, whips and swirls, the artificial puddings, nondairy "creaming agents," the "cheese foods" such as Velveeta, the cream pies and pastries, Kool-Aid, Tang, Hi-C and Yoo-Hoo.

The advanced course covers collage and sculptural materials such as luncheon meats, white breads, frozen waffles and ethnic foods. All aspects of painting will be covered, from color, form and composition to still life, model, landscape and various abstract styles. The advanced course also includes mixed media, such as food videotapes.

#33479–KEEPING BEES IN A CIGAR BOX
(Wed., 9:00, $20)
Hal Tinsley

The bee is one of the toughest, most resilient and forgiving creatures in the insect kingdom, and of course, one of the most productive for mankind. Contrary to popular belief, the bee can exist under the most difficult conditions and still provide his proper share of honey. Keeping

Hobbies 27

bees in a cigar box is the ideal method for the city apartment dweller who lacks the requisite space for a complete bee house. As many as five hundred bees can be kept in a single standard-size cigar container as long as they are carefully watched and cultivated.

Hal Tinsley, author of *1001 Bees in a Box*, gives you invaluable instruction on how to raise bees in this restricted space without suffering the loss of a single specimen. You'll learn how to shake your box correctly to prevent the bees from sticking to each other, how to keep your bees busy, how to discern when they are cranky and need to be fed, (bees like tiny bites of anchovy, tuna and minced chives), and most important, how to administer the special bee tranquilizers that keep them in a relaxed, laid-back mood despite their cramped conditions.

#69842—SANDWICH MAKING WORKSHOPS
(Saturday, 4:00, $35)
Nina Ginglia, Sandy Ditz

Cooking styles may come and go, but nothing replaces the sandwich as the all-time most popular food in America. Yet there are millions of people who take the sandwich for granted, not knowing what a rich, gastronomically exciting world they are missing. Here in a series of intensive workshop courses, you can master the many arts of sandwich making from the fundamentals to the *haute* sandwiches of the stars.

Sandwich Workshop 1.1
NINA GINGLIA

While most people know that a sandwich consists of a food filling between two pieces of bread, they know very little else. This course starts with the bare basics, assuming you know nothing. Nina Ginglia, head sandwich chef at Val's Luncheonette, discusses every aspect of the art, beginning with utensils, the various breads and the basic fillings, such as cold cuts, cheeses, processed fish, meats, eggs and fowl recipes. You will learn the proper proportions for each filling, how to garnish with lettuce, tomato and other vegetables, how to use condiments and dressings, how to toast breads properly, how to cut sandwiches without the fillings squirting out, which fillings "marry" best with others and much more.

In the second part of the course you will learn how to make the classic three from which most of today's sandwich cuisines are derived—the simple grills (ham or bacon with cheeses), the mixtures of cold cuts, cheeses and vegetables, the various salads (tuna, ham, chicken, egg), hot varieties and the more complex combinations of double and triple deckers. You'll learn techniques of "dressing up" a sandwich with "garni" and a specially useful section will be devoted to rejuvenating leftovers and creating hot "open" sandwiches.

Sandwich Workshop 1.2
SANDY DITZ

This course specializes in the new "lighter" sandwich cuisines, the controversial *Sandwich Nouvelle* and *Sandwich Minceur* championed by the Young Turks of the sandwich world led by Gus Trikinosis, the Bloom Brothers and Michael Dago. Sandy Ditz, the successful owner of Sandy's Sandwich Shop, has had many years of amateur and professional experience and is one of the foremost teachers of both schools.

Essentially, the Nouvelle Sandwich School attempts to redefine the ingredients and flavors of the sandwich, combining what seem to be incompatible flavors. The results, when they are successful, are spectacular. Sometimes a *Sandwich Nouvelle* can be deceptively simple and gets its offbeat flavor from a dash of Karo syrup or a quick squeeze of a well-used dishrag. It relies primarily on simplicity and the remarkable combination of pristinely fresh ingredients and offbeat condiments. Among others, you will learn how to make such sandwiches as thinly sliced raw pork with leeks and pomegranates, steamed mussels with kiwi and cilantro, and julienne of trout skins with marrow and blue peppercorns.

Sandwich Minceur, on the other hand, is even more concerned with lightness and is especially important for dieters. Here is where you'll learn how to create new low-sodium, low-cholesterol ingredients and offbeat substitutes for the more traditional, heavier condiments and breads. You'll learn how to use the new food processors to create new and dazzling sandwiches such as eggwhite and mustard seed mousse on low-sodium whole wheat wafers, cucumber loaf with three kinds of lettuce and cold raw cod with sesame and pecans.

Sandwich Workshop 1.3
SANDY DITZ

Now that you've learned the basics, the classics and the lighter cuisines, you are ready to branch out into the ethnic specialties, the famous celebrity recipes, party and catering style sandwiches and the improvisational workshop. Sandy Ditz gives you her own variations on these ethnic types: the Hero or Submarine, the Near Eastern pita sandwiches, the Jewish bagel specialties and some elegant French varieties.

Emphasis is on perfect proportions and proper mixing of ingredients, which in some cases number up to fifteen in one sandwich: Nick Hercules, the short-order man at Sandy's own shop, will provide instruction in professional high-speed sandwich making, showing you how to organize your ingredients, how to make as many as twelve items at once, how to master advanced cutting techniques and the colorful short-order-cook vocabulary.

The celebrity sandwich section will feature some of the all-time favorite combinations favored by stars of films and TV, including the Elvis (cheeseburger, fries, chili dog and caviar), the John Lennon (tuna, refried beans, and sauerkraut), the Victoria Principal (ham, macaroni and cherries) and the Robin Williams (Italian salami, corn flakes, broccoli leaf and calves foot jelly).

In conclusion there will be a fun-filled "improv" session where you will be given a batch of ingredients and asked to create your own original sandwiches from scratch, in a matter of minutes. Your improvisations will be judged by Nina, Sandy and Nick. Prizes will be awarded to the three best sandwiches and they will be featured for an entire week at Sandy's Sandwich Shop.

#96834—VOYEURING
(Tues, 9:00, $35)
Max Resnick, George Pachinko

Once just a pleasant pastime with slightly perverse overtones, voyeuring is now considered a healthy form of emotional release and an imaginative way to create a rewarding fantasy life. In its more advanced forms, this activity could lead you to a well-paying, exciting new career in the field of Criminal Surveillance and Investigation.

Max Resnick, a veteran voyeur and former security guard for the Otis Elevator Corporation, discusses the simpler forms of voyeurism: the old-fashioned Na-

---

● BUY A CHARTER MEMBERSHIP IN OUR GOLDEN LIFETIME STUDENT PLAN ●

Take an unlimited number of courses for the rest of your life, all at one astoundingly low price. A once in a lifetime offer! For prices, see Sal, room 443, Mon–Sat, 6 PM to midnight, or call 688-3434.

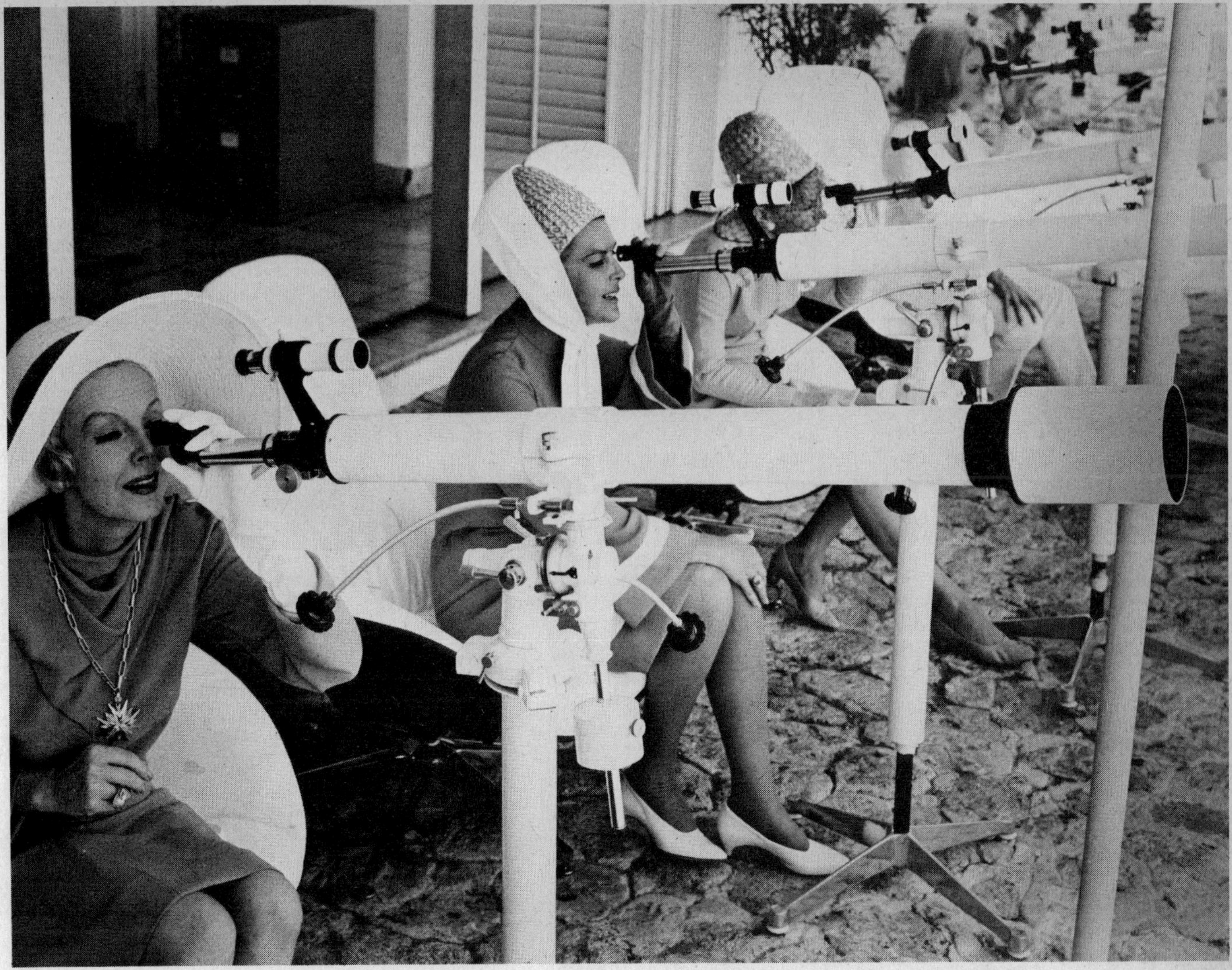

OVER-EXTENSION UNIVERSITY BULLETIN

ked Eye Technique, the binocular method, also known as "Birdwatching" and the High-powered Telescope Technique, or "Surveying the Stars."

You will learn how to conceal yourself, how to use sophisticated optical equipment and most important, how to find suitable "love objects" for your particular needs, whether they are single, or in a couple or multiples.

George Pachinko will follow with a special seminar on turning your pastime into a rewarding new career outlining the opportunities awaiting you in the booming field of criminal surveillance. Qualified students can elect to take Mr. Pachinko's advanced course in this area.

Related Courses in Hobbies

How to Make Costume Jewelry Out of Szechuan Food, #43861
How to Make Your Own Paper Shopping Bags, #42845
Computer Carpentry, #41829
Plastic Surgery for Amateurs, #40806
P.S. Your Mother Is Dead: How to Create Imaginative Practical Jokes, #39782

Hobbies 29

OVER-EXTENSION UNIVERSITY BULLETIN

GOT A MINUTE GOT A MINUTE GOT A

All courses are one dollar for one minute. No substitutions are permitted.

#01–HOW TO SCRATCH YOUR BODY PROPERLY
(Fri., Noon, $1)
Seymour Tokay

Scratching your body is both a pleasure and a necessity. Unfortunately, very few people know how to achieve the maximum pleasure and rewards. Seymour Tokay demonstrates various scratching techniques and strokes, shows you how to scratch perfectly with blunt fingernails, how to use scratching tools, how to perform erotic scratches and most important, he will show you how to scratch those difficult-to-reach parts of your own body without strain. Each student will receive a free sample of Mr. Tokay's own skin lotion, which will be used during the course.

#02–HOW TO BATHE AND SHOWER PROPERLY
(Mon., Noon, $1)
Seymour Bupp

Many people do not get the most out of their daily bathing and showering because they have never been taught basic techniques. Seymour Bupp has been taking showers and baths for over thirty-five years—twenty of these in his own *personal* tub—and offers many insights into this neglected area. Learn how to select the proper water temperature, how to choose the soap that is right for your skin, how to soap your body properly (the crotch method, the body swirl). You'll learn practical and *sensual* scrubbing techniques, which parts of your body should be cleaned more thoroughly, and how to rinse. There will also be a survey of shampooing methods and brief instruction on toweling and bathtub hygiene.

#03–HIGH-SPEED HAIR DRYING
(Wed., Noon, $1)
Larry LaSeur

Many people are unable or are afraid to harness the heating power of the high setting on their hair dryers. But once you've mastered this technique you can blow dry with the confidence and speed of a professional. Learn quick curling, fluffing and natural teasing, all in a minute or less.

#04–MASTERING YOUR CLOCK RADIO
(Thurs., Noon, $1)
Jack Schvitzer

Delve into the ultra-sophisticated electronic world of clock radios including the new digital and computer-operated models. Learn how to "scan" for the music and news stations, how to adjust volume and tone controls and how to set the alarm for the exact time, right to the second. Start your mornings on the perfect note. You'll never wake up to the wrong music or the wrong time again.

#05–HOW TO COOK A MINUTE STEAK
(Tues., Noon, $1)
Bob Bushmeyer

If you own a watch you can learn how to cook a scrumptious steak. It's just a matter of timing and knowing when to turn the meat over. A great way to meet that certain someone who likes his meat fast and sizzling hot.

#06–SPEED LISTENING
(Fri., Noon, $1)
Jeffrey Pushberg

After speedwriting and speed reading there is an even more important new learning discipline—speed listening—the science of picking up and understanding what your friend, lover, relative, etc. is telling you in seconds, and anticipating his conversation for minutes to come, so you can form a well-reasoned, intelligent answer to his conversation. Jeffrey Pushberg, author of *Stop, Look, and For God's Sake, Listen,* will show you how to listen quickly, the shortcuts to a person's point of view, and how to "read" what he is really saying no matter what he is saying out loud.

#07–HOW TO OPEN A RAW CLAM
(Tues., Noon, $1)
Ted Mann

Many people are totally helpless in the art of opening or "shucking" a raw clam. Ted Mann, a veteran clam shucker at one of the most famous seafood restaurants in the city, shows you his quick, easy twist of the wrist method for opening clams that will end your frustration and bloody palms forever. Bring your own clams.

#08–TOP DUSTING
(Wed., Noon, $1)
Janice Flannel

Top dusting is the name given to the science of cleaning household surfaces, especially furniture. With the air pollution problem growing more dangerous every day, the amount of dust and bacteria that settle on furniture tops has increased over 4000 percent since 1970. Janice Flannel, an expert in cleaning materials and furniture waxes, discusses what types of cleansers, sprays and waxes can do the right cleaning and dusting job for you, "regardless of what the TV commercials say," says Ms. Flannel.

#09–GUM TASTING
(Mon., Noon, $1)
Harvey Wall

With the dazzling variety of gum available today the dedicated chewer is often bewildered by the choices and options. Should he try the fruity types that offer a quick flavor hit but often lack staying power, or should he pick one of the minty types that seem to have a more steady, balanced flavor over a longer period. And what about diet gums? Are there any brands that can truly satisfy the serious chewer? Harvey Wall, a professional gum chewer gives you an honest, factual survey of the many brands, with starred ratings for the ones he thinks are "worth a detour to find" or are "best buys."

#010–BELTS OR SUSPENDERS?
(Thurs., Noon, $1)
Myron Hanker

Most men do not realize how good they would look if they switched to wearing suspenders instead of a belt. Myron Hanker gives you an instant Waistline Analysis to determine whether you are a Beltomorph or Suspendomorph. He will then recommend the perfect type of belt or suspender for your needs.

OVER-EXTENSION UNIVERSITY BULLETIN

NUTE GOT A MINUTE GOT A MINUTE

#011–HOW TO FIND YOUR MISSING CONTACT LENS
(Tues., Noon, $1)
Murray Lapel

Murray Lapel shows contact lens owners a foolproof method for finding a dropped lens, no matter what kind of surface it lands on. Mr. Lapel guarantees you will find your missing lens, even if you drop it on the beach. Avoid unnecessary replacements, save money, save all those hours of endless searching.

#012–HOW TO PLAY CHOPSTICKS
(Wed., Noon, $1)
Nina Scarf

If you've always dreamed of playing the piano but were frightened by the idea of learning to read music and taking lessons, this is your chance to master a popular tune in seconds, a tune that you can play over and over again at parties, alone or with a partner. Nina Scarf, an accomplished pianist, will guide your hands over the keyboard and show you how to memorize the piano "map" so you can play this song anywhere.

#017–HOW TO REVIVE A USED BALL POINT PEN
(Thurs., Noon, $1)
Spencer Colon

Every year millions of perfectly usable ball point pens are thrown away because their owners thought they were dried up and unusable. The fact is, most ball point pens can be used indefinitely if you know the secret of how to tap their hidden reservoir of unused ink. Mr. Colon, a former executive with the Bic Corporation, shows you how it's done—saving you hundreds a year in stationery expenses.

#018–HOW TO SHAKE HANDS
(Tues., Noon, $1)
Leonard Stoones

Nothing can turn off a new business prospect or a new lover faster than the wrong handshake. Leonard Stoones, a maître d' in one of the city's busiest restaurants, has perfected the perfect handshake—not too firm, not too limp. He'll also show you how to prevent sweaty palms, how to shake hands with a sexual overtone, how to "intimidate" someone with a normal "smooth" handshake and much more.

#019–CHEAP COOKIES
(Mon., Noon, $1)
Seymour Kartel

Everybody loves cookies but with today's soaring inflation and rising prices it's becoming increasingly difficult to find a decent cookie for under $5 a pound. Seymour Kartel has scoured the inexpensive cookie sections of over 50 supermarkets and has tasted virtually every type and every brand. In a lively tasting and analysis he will guide you to the Top 20 cookies in town, none higher than $1.29 for a 12 oz. package!

#020–MAKE YOURSELF DOUBLE-JOINTED
(Fri., Noon, $1)
Bonnie Ditz

People who are double-jointed are able to do more difficult physical stunts than ordinary folk. They can also be the life of the party with their "funny fingers" performing all sorts of odd tricks. Yet the truth is, most of them weren't born with this talent, they had to learn it. Bonnie Ditz, a physical therapist, has developed a simple muscle control exercise that will turn your fingers and toes into twenty little dancers.

#021–HOW TO MAKE TRANSATLANTIC TELEPHONE CALLS
(Thurs., Noon, $1)
Seymour Kartel

Long distance calls, especially to foreign lands, can be difficult and annoying to make if you don't know how. Mr. Kartel will show you the short cuts, the quick dial systems, the money-saving times to call and much more, guaranteeing you better, cheaper transatlantic and transpacific calls. One lucky student will be chosen by lot to make a real call, free.

#022–HOW TO POUR BEER
(Tues., Noon, $1)
Barney Jerski

The neglected art of beer pouring is revived with great flair and expertise by Barney Jerski, a retired bartender and veteran beer drinker. Mr. Jerski shows you how to get an extra large foamy head, a large head, medium, and if you really like it, a small thin head. Bring a six pack or more of your favorite brand and share them with Barney.

#023–CATCH A NEW LOVER WITH A FISHING ROD
(Fri., Noon, $1)
Joanna Bushing

A new way to cope with the singles scene that is both refreshing and effective. Find the person that looks like "Mr. or Ms. Right," cast out your line and hook your "fish." It's all done with Joanna Bushing's delightful "miniature" fishing rod that comes equipped with a harmless hook that has a small, clever ice-breaking message attached ot it. The casting technique is as easy as playing "Ring Toss." Your little rod folds up like an umbrella and can be taken anywhere you think you can find a new lover.

#024–WHERE TO FIND THE FUNNIEST T-SHIRTS
(Tues., Noon, $1)
Jack Putrell

You always attract attention and make new friends easily by wearing a "novelty" t-shirt that has a funny saying on it. Most of the best t-shirt sayings are written by the Irish. Jack Putrell will relate over fifty of the funniest Irish t-shirt lines to you, each one suitable for wearing, and he will advise on where to get them made for a reasonable price.

● EXCLUSIVE MONEY-BACK GUARANTEE IF YOU DO NOT FIND A NEW LOVER ●

Your tuition fees will be cheerfully refunded if you do not find a new lover in one of your courses.

Got A Minute   31

SOCIAL ADVENTURES

THE GREAT OUTDOORS

#75291–WINO TOURS
(Fridays, $25)
Norman Trueberger

Every city has a colorful, raffish skid row neighborhood, an area where down and out derelicts, hobos and winos like to hang out, discuss "What went wrong," and figure out ways to survive through another day.

Norman Trueberger, who is both an urban planner and a wine expert, takes you on a carefully planned tour where you'll meet some of the most fascinating men and women of our time who are now unfortunate dropouts from society. You can "interview" them, enjoy their unusual "takes" on society and share a bottle of their favorite wine or whiskey. At the same time, Mr. Trueberger will point out the many forgotten architectural landmarks in this "wino country" area.

You'll meet writers, athletes, detectives, musicians and career military men, who were once in high- and middle-level management all with wonderful stories to tell—yarns full of melodrama, pathos, tragedy and dark humor. Don't forget to bring a little loose change.

#66348–SINGLES TRAFFIC JAMS
The New Way to Find a Lover
(Fri., 7:30, $40)
Larry Luccione

The traffic jam has become one of the most profound semiotic symbols of modern living, a problem that becomes more oppressive every day. This course will show you how to deal with this dilemma in a new and exciting way, turning an unsolvable problem into a rich and rewarding experience.

Larry Luccione, a former traffic policeman and bartender, will discuss a new social phenomenon, the Singles Traffic Jam, and how it can change your life.

The Singles Traffic Jam arose initially out of sheer necessity, as thousands of cars were stuck in the long rush-hour lines. Delays and tie-ups were so prolonged that the drivers and passengers formed ad hoc social groups. Communication between cars was easy, especially in good weather, with windows and sunroofs open. It was inevitable that people with similar interests would find themselves "back to back" on the congested highways every day, and many of them became friends and lovers. Car hopping was common and soon little impromptu "bars" were set up so that friendships could be explored more deeply as the cars crawled slowly along the clogged arteries of our outmoded traffic system.

Mr. Luccione will discuss where to find the most attractive young singles in traffic jams, where to get stuck if you want to meet certain types—such as doctors, dentists, engineers, models, actresses; how to break into the cliques; where to find the most expensive cars (for upscale high income prospects) and much more. Most important, he will show you how to break away from a traffic jam and find a shortcut when "creeps" and oddballs try to force their way in.

#00751–ZOO SAFARIS
Hunting Animals Behind Bars
(Sat., 3:30, $40)
Barney Zingara

For sheer excitement and high drama nothing can compare to an African safari. Unfortunately, the costs of a safari are far beyond the means of most of us. But now there is a chance to capture many of the same thrills right near your home for a nominal fee.

By special arrangement with the officials of one of our largest, best-stocked zoos, we will be allowed to hunt and kill certain animals who are extremely ill and would ordinarily be put to sleep. Indeed, the current zoological theories are more in favor of this kind of death for terminally sick animals, as it gives them the nostalgic feeling of returning to their original wild state.

With the guidance of Barney Zingara, a former travel agent who worked in Nairobi, we will simulate the same conditions and atmosphere of a genuine African safari. You will be picked up in a Land Rover, driven to the zoo, where a Negro "bearer" will carry your bags and help you load your rifle. Mr. Zingara will instruct you on the nature of the terrain and how to stalk your prey. It is important to remember that we cannot guarantee which animals will be available for shooting. Naturally, many aspiring hunters would like to bag a lion or a tiger, but sometimes the only animals ready for termination are monkeys. We will be notified in advance as to which animals we can shoot.

Your safari adventure also includes a lunch cooked outdoors by one of the bearers, a high-powered rifle and one box of free bullets (more ammunition is available at a nominal cost). For those who cannot bring themselves to hunt, there are excellent cameras for rent. Mr. Zingara can also arrange for reasonably priced taxidermy for any animal credited to you.

#57812–WILDERNESS HIKE THROUGH THE SLUMS
(Fridays, 7:00, $20)
Rafael "Skull" Sanchez

Tired of trekking up rugged mountain paths and wet, muddy forest trails? Get back to your city roots with a fascinating backpacking trip through a legendary slum neighborhood. See the remains of the Great Fires and Bombings of the 60s and 70s, ruins that equal those of Pompeii and Greece. Bring your camera and photograph the wild dogs and graceful brown rats of a major boulevard. The hike includes a stopover at a pimp bar, a heroin "shooting gallery" and a Social Club where you can mingle with attractive, exotic Latinos and dance to their savage rhythms.

URBAN ADVENTURES

#75116–BASEMENT FUN
Getting the Most Out of Your Basement
(Tues., 7:30, $25)
Barry Beaverman

Sometimes called "the most neglected room in the house," the basement is finally coming into its own as an important living unit in our contemporary society. Millions of homeowners and many condominium and apartment dwellers have access to this space and for the most part have not developed the basement to its fullest potential as a source of recreation, fun and games.

This course shows you how to decorate your basement in various styles—"the sportsman," with hunting and fishing motifs, the "intellectual or artiste," with shelves of books, the "hobbyist" (workshop table, etc.), the "connoisseur of wine and spirits" (bar, wine racks, etc.) and many, many more. If none of these looks are right for you there is also the popular "rec room" which lends itself to any activity.

You will learn how to use your basement to rejuvenate your social relationships. For instance, you can spend the night in the basement with your loved one, or "get away from it all" for an entire weekend. Simply make believe you're staying at the Holiday Inn or Hilton. Have your food delivered (room service!), watch TV in bed in perfect peace and quiet.

Many basement party ideas with kooky "themes" will be discussed. For instance, if you like "black humor" perhaps you'll give a basement party to celebrate Albert Speer's birthday. You'll have your friends chuckling and roaring as you decorate your basement with German flags and swastikas and greet them in an SS or Luftwaffe uniform. Serve plenty of fine German food and beer. And to show that it's all just tongue in cheek, rig up a dart board with a picture of the Fuhrer on it and have everyone throw their darts at it.

A special section of the course is devoted to the apartment house dweller, including how to meet singles in basements and how to dress for basement fun.

At the conclusion of the course we will have our own gala basement party with canapes, munchies and a professional disco tape cassette. BYOB!

Social Adventures 33

#19365–SCRATCH 'N' SNIFF SINGLES PARTIES
(Saturdays, 9-ish, $20)
Bruce Kogl

Bruce Kogl of Bruce Kogl Enterprises, is one of the country's leading developers of "scratch 'n' sniff" products, those items made with specially processed papers that exude familiar smells when you scratch them with your fingernail.

Mr. Kogl has organized a group of cocktail parties for singles that will feature lively contests, special entertainment and fun-filled surprises, all designed around his novelty scratch 'n' sniff products including Blind Fold Guess the Odor contests, Scratch 'n' Sniff Bingo and Scratch 'n' Sniff Mock Strip Poker.

These parties are tailored for men and women with a zany sense of humor who want to meet new friends and lovers in an atmosphere of uninhibited fun.

Free refreshments and plenty of good music will be offered. Dress any way you like, but come with an open mind, a free spirit and sharp fingernails!

#69111–TAKE A MIDNIGHT TOUR WITH A PRIVATE GARBAGE CARTING COMPANY
(Sat., Midnight, $50)
Pepi Scumbazzo

One of the most offbeat and least known jobs in urban areas is the work of the private garbage carting companies, the truck drivers who work "round 'bout midnight" and beyond, collecting the garbage from restaurants, night clubs, discos and bars. Many carting company drivers have gained "entrée" to these glamorous, raffish night spots as guests, attaining the status of a new breed of underground sex symbols. With their newfound notoriety, they are mingling easily with celebrated rock and film stars, politicians, models, power brokers and other famous "night people" in the exciting after-hours hangouts they service.

With your host, carting company driver Pepi Scumbazzo, you and a carefully selected group of like-minded, adventurous people will tour these nocturnal haunts. You'll watch the garbage being collected and join Pepi when he's invited inside to "play." You'll "hang out" with genuine jet setters and millionaires, kinky rock stars and models, famous actors and actresses in their "private" clubs. You'll also meet colorful "loft dwellers," unusual and creative freelance artists, writers, musicians and designers whose real nightlife begins after midnight—people with exotic, offbeat ideas in food, clothes, sex and politics—people whose ideas may not jibe with yours, but who are capable of stimulating you and giving you a new perspective for the future.

Pepi Scumbazzo, a close friend of Frank Sinatra, promises you a night of fun and surprises you'll never forget—a night to make new friends, meet new lovers and have the time of your life. You might want to take a nap earlier in the day so you can be bright-eyed and perky for this nocturnal romp!

#13250–HOW TO MEET UNUSUAL NEW LOVERS
(Wed., 9:00, $30)
Donna Twidzik

How many times have you heard an attractive, intelligent woman lament about her boredom and frustration with the men she meets? Why do so many women feel shackled and imprisoned in their day-to-day lives? Why are so many women indulging in the impossible fantasies found in cheap romantic novels? The answer is simple: Most of the men they meet *are* dull and ordinary.

Even though many women are content with normal "straight" men as friends and lovers, a growing number are far more dissatisfied and are looking for more stimulation and excitement from the "offbeat" men, men who do not fall into any well-defined category because of their unique, strongly developed lifestyles.

Ms. Twidzik discusses the many types of lovers available, their pluses and minuses and matches you to your most compatible type. For starters, there is the "kooky" male, the daffy, zany type usually found in small, improvisational comedy nightclubs and kosher style delicatessen restaurants. Then, there are eccentrics (usually harmless, sometimes rich) found in literary bars that cater to rich WASPS and bisexuals.

From kooks, harmless eccentrics and dilettantes it's a natural step to the more "dangerous" eccentrics and "outlaw" types, such as ex-convicts and drug dealers. For the truly adventurous, Ms. Twidzik discusses where to find part-time criminals, full-time criminals, psychopaths, sexual deviates and other unusual, fascinating men.

You will discover where these men congregate, how to attract them, how to live with and cope with their problems and most important, how to break off a relationship when it becomes too dangerous.

The three most important qualities to look for in offbeat men are wealth, a sense of high drama and just enough eccentricity to make your life more fascinating and adventurous, without making you too tense or over-stimulated. Donna Twidzik shows you how it can be done.

#98111–LEATHER AND CHEESE PARTIES
(Thurs., 10:00, $50)
Stan and Vicki Groover

A perfect setting to create new, offbeat relationships and explore an exciting juxtaposition of physical pleasures. This course combines the tactile sensuality of

OVER-EXTENSION UNIVERSITY BULLETIN

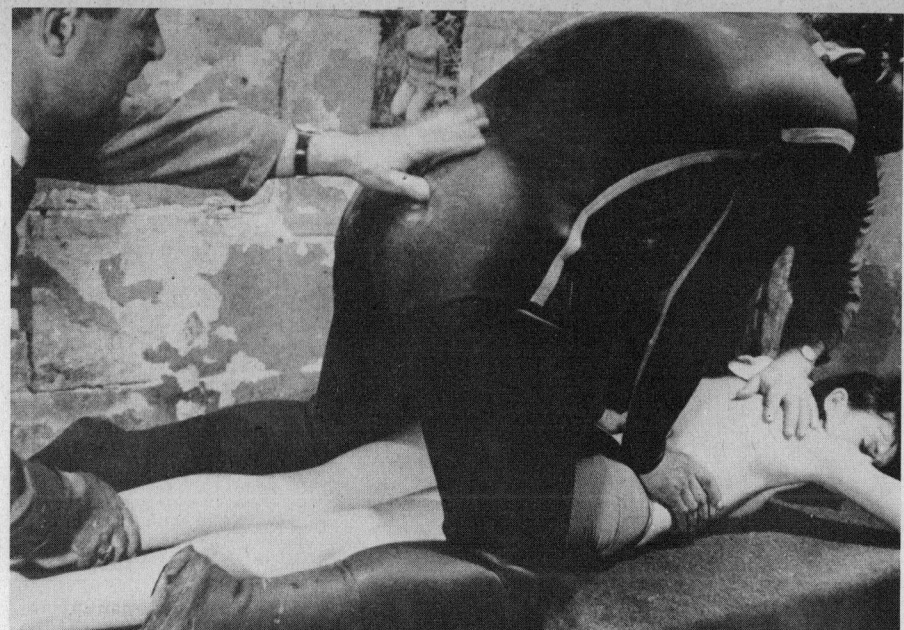

● REMEMBER: YOU CAN REGISTER FOR ANY COURSE, ANY TIME. IF YOU REGISTER IN THE MIDDLE OF A COURSE, TAKE IT AGAIN THROUGH THE PART YOU MISSED ●

leather with the gastronomic satisfaction of cheese eating in a smart, fashionable party setting. The requirements are simple: You must dress completely in leather and bring your favorite cheese. Crackers and beverages are complimentary.

The sight, smells and textures of rich, genuine leather clothing are a perfect marriage to the joys of eating ripe, pungent, delicious cheeses. Leather and cheese create an aura of sensuality that elevates an ordinary party into a dramatic experience, a chance to connect with a new lover or friend on a deeper, more visceral level. In today's fast-moving world, who has time for anything superficial? At the same time you will have the opportunity to taste many new interesting cheeses and discover many new wardrobe ideas. A list of cheese recommendations will be given free before the course starts. No vinyl, naugahyde or other imitation leather garments are allowed. No cottage cheese, plain cream cheese, Velveeta or other packaged process cheeses will be accepted. We are looking forward to clothing of pure, luxurious leather and gourmet cheeses from many lands to enhance this unique experiment in social relations.

#28106–JUGS AND JOINTS PARTY
(Sat. Midnite, $25)
Rip Carver

One of the most cherished memories of the 60s was your first marijuana and jug wine party, when everyone was experimenting with new lifestyles and new ways to "blow their minds." It was a time of hope, a time of liberation and a time to just have a good time.

Rip Carver, "a child of the 60s" and a veteran of many "J and J" parties re-creates the J and J party for the 80s, capturing the essence of its old charm and adding a bright, new sophisticated touch for those whose tastes have become more refined and mature.

Mr. Carver will show you how to plan your J and J party, whether it's for two or two hundred—how to handle the buying of refreshments, the "munchies," and of course, the drugs.* You'll learn how to enhance the mood of the party with special decor tricks, music and costumes. You'll plan everything from a "bring your own" party to a slick, high-powered affair that will make a Hollywood producer purple with envy!

You'll learn the basics of judging good "grass," how to find trustworthy sources, how to spot a "narc" and what jug wines go best with your grass. Most important, you will create parties where you can relax and get "high" with compatible, intelligent people who share your interests and ideas—bright professionals who want to "break the emotional ice" and develop new meaningful relationships in a mellow, "with it" atmosphere that will promote feelings of warmth and emotional communication.

* We neither condone nor condemn the use of marijuana, but we do recognize that it has become an accepted and highly popular drug among law abiding citizens, including many of our most respected public figures. Medical authorities do not have the final word on this controversial drug at this moment. As far as we know, it does no irreparable harm if taken in moderation.

Related Courses in Social Adventures

URBAN ADVENTURES

50s Petting and Necking Parties, #64325

Weekend Fun: Take a Trip to an Industrial Park and Find a New Lover, #63319

Achieve Instant Intimacy Through Genital Grabbing, #62304

Indoor Picnics: All the Fun Without the Insects, #61305

Singles Suicide Seminar and Wine Tasting Parties, #60297

How to Find a Lover in a Laundromat, #56281

Dental Flossing Parties: a New Way to Meet a Lover, #55275

Blindfolded Bus Rides: Take a One-Way Trip to Nowhere and Find a New Lover, #54261

OUTDOOR ADVENTURES

Logging in the Wilds: Cut Down Your Own Trees in a National Park, #58291

Rooftop Fun, #57285

● ALL MAJOR DOMESTIC AND FOREIGN CREDIT CARDS ARE ACCEPTED ●

THE PERFORMING ARTS

MUSIC

#65107–THE SILVER AGE OF JAZZ
Lesser-Known Groups of the 20s, 30s and 40s
(Wed., 9:00, $25)
Barney Kitzel

Any jazz fan is fully acquainted with the nationally famous big bands, small groups and vocalists, but few are familiar with the groups that were regional favorites, groups that performed in one area, such as the midwest or the south. There were hundreds of these groups active from the early 20s up to World War II—dance bands, Dixieland bands, big, hot swinging bands, small jazz combos, vocal-instrumental groups, novelty "Mickey Mouse" bands, even some avant-garde jazz groups. They played in such colorful places as the Muskrat Lounge in Dayton, the Riff-Raff Room of the Hotel Montmorency in Moline, the Purple Penguin in Cleveland and many more.

Unfortunately, most of these groups never made recordings, but Barney Kitzel, a noted jazz historian and author of *Hog Mouth: The Biography of Ernest "Hog Mouth" Tibbs*, the quadriplegic jazz harmonica player, has amassed hundreds of interviews with surviving bandleaders and musicians and will re-create this happy, innocent age when everyone was making wonderful music.

Here are just a few of the groups that will be discussed: Ben Boney and his Davenport Sitters, Don Bongo, Billy "Bubbles" Bundlestein, Sam Borscht and his Seven Beets, Georgie Bizarre, Clarence "Jugboat" Browne, Ted Broadstairs, Bobby Bee and the Honeymakers, Baron Billington, Box Biederbier, Nelson Bandolier, Chubby Choquette, the Joe Cuervo Trio, Nick Casaba, Don Dixie and the Debonaires, The Finn Sisters ("Laff and Coff"), Frankie Fargo, Wayne Glade and his Glidin' Rhythms, Harry Hudson and his Hawaiian Hoosiers, Marion Hochleiter, Hal Harbinger, Nat Hesseltine, Ray Humberstone, Jimmy Jethro and his Garbage Pickers, the Buster Jones Jam-Tette, Lee Lebow and his Jewish Gypsies, The Lee Sisters ("Ugh and Beast"), Lonnie LeMay and his Lounge Lizards, Art Loam, Henry "Lullaby" Lester, Jack Levantine, Gene LaSalle, the vocalist Lyn Lovely, Snazzy LaPierre and his Slowpokes, Brad Lillywhite and his Sooner Serenaders, Henry Mabuse, Tito Miramar, Nat Millstein, Mal Malentine and his Mosey Along Masqueraders, Babs Malone, Betty Muggles, Shorty Maraschino and his Cherry Pitters, Sy Novotny, Orville O'Vay and his Old Time Oldies, Pete Potero's Plum Pruners, Red Pemminger, Sonny Simmons and his Sinning Syncopators, Stan Shlumberger and his Shady Ladies, Butch St. Clair, Bernie Sylvester and his vocalist wife, Nina Nonay, Vito Storm (nee Stromboli), Orlando Tampa and his Tallahasseans, Tiny Tremaine, Benny "Blue Baby" Timms, Tony Tone and his Torrid Ten, Floyd Teaks, The Tivoli Brothers, Tommy and Jimmy, Rudy Tapas, Del Toronado, Lew Turniquet and his Band-Aids, Dick Weisenheimer, Van Winkerly and his Winkie Blinks, Kyle Woodburner, Will Williams and his Waco Wailers, and Ira Zinfandel, who ended just about every list of big bands.

#74976–THE SLANG OF ROCK AND ROLL
(Thurs., 9:00, $25)
Frank Rose

Frank Rose, a leading popular music critic, social historian and former roadie will discuss the evolution of Rock and Roll slang and attempt to define the best and longest-lasting examples—though slang is admittedly a risky area for making definitive judgments. Students will learn many of the latest slang words and phrases, many of which are still part of the "underground" counter-culture, such as "mowing the lawn" (making lots of money), "shoe horn" (stingy promoter), "Dandruff" (cocaine and other white powdered drugs), "Shampoo" (to go straight, to give up dandruff, as in "I'm going to shampoo myself"), "boxcar" (a female hanger-on, formerly called a "groupie"), "guppy" (a small, underage groupie, jailbait), "beef"—noun (a great musician, i.e., "He's a beef." Adjective—"He's real beefy"), "chocolate chip" (a hit record).

As part of the course Mr. Rose will conduct several visits to the backstages of various concerts where we will eavesdrop on actual rock and roll groups during their live performances in the hope of catching some of their unique slang.

#11554–100 YEARS OF GREEK JAZZ
(Mon., 7:30, $25)
Pete Manilla

The Greeks invented tragedy and they probably invented jazz as well. Long before the Negroes sang the blues, the Greeks were playing and singing *kibi*, the sometimes mournful, sometimes happy music of the olive pickers. Kibi was a mixture of field hollers, shepherd's trills, and syncopation that was soon picked up by the taverna musicians, who melded it into their own semi-improvisational songs and produced the form we know as Greek jazz. Our course will offer a detailed study of the odyssey of the kibi and how it finally ended up in the Greek dance clubs and the Greek diners, where jazz concerts were usually performed in the slack periods between lunch and dinner.

Special attention will be given to the works of such Greek jazz greats as Louis

"Satchmo" Armagannis, Jellyroll Pappas, Dizzy Costas, Charley "Yardbird" Pappalapoulous, Miles Darvas, Count Trikonis and "Fats" Dukasis. Our final class will feature live performances by guest Greek jazz artists. Retsina and cheese will be served in a cabaret-like atmosphere.

#16543–THE GOLDEN AGE OF SEMICLASSICAL MUSIC
(Tues., 7:30, $15)
Stanley Vermin

Stanley Vermin will analyze the peak creative era of semiclassical music, the 50s—as exemplified in the recordings of Mantovani, Percy Faith and the Melachrino Strings. He will analyze and illustrate the typical Mantovani musical arrangement, the importance of the viola and other lower register strings in the Melachrino orchestra and the groundbreaking string and chorus work of Percy Faith and Ray Conniff. Each of these recording artist's greatest hits will be played and discussed. At the final class the widows of Mantovani and Melachrino will be our special guests, reminiscing about their husbands and relating many fascinating anecdotes about their personal as well as their musical lives.

#98624–HOW TO STAY AWAKE AT THE OPERA
(Wed., 7:30, $40)
Murray Skirmish

For most people brought up watching movies and TV a visit to the opera can be a difficult experience. Although the music is intermittently catchy, the plots are usually silly, the singers are overweight and unattractive and the production is nearly always static and unimaginative. All this

---

• **ATTENTION MEMBERS OF LABOR UNIONS, FRATERNAL ORDERS, CHARITY ORGANIZATIONS, PRIVATE CLUBS AND SOCIETIES** •

Ask for our special group rates. See Viola in room 439.

makes it very difficult to stay awake after about ten minutes of the first act.

This course will deal in complete detail with all strategies and tactics of opera going: how to stay awake, how to look like an aficionado, even certain surefire critical phrases that will stamp you as an expert.

The first section of the course deals with food and drink—namely, the pros and cons of having dinner and drinks before or after the opera. Mr. Skirmish will outline the advantages and disadvantages of both strategies. For most opera goers, the best idea is a snack before the opera and a light après-opera dinner, although there's no foolproof way to avoid total slumber during the performance. If you eat before, you'll be full and sluggish. If you eat after, you'll be starving and cranky during the performance, your stomach will rumble, and you'll fall asleep dreaming about food.

The main part of the course deals with how to stay awake. Some of the ideas that will be discussed are daydreaming without sleeping, sex fantasies without embarrassing erections, the art of pinching yourself, the art of punching yourself, using your companion as an elbow jabber to keep you awake and much more.

Mr. Skirmish guarantees to teach you how to stay awake—or, at the very least, how to appear awake—how to avoid a dead sleep with embarrassing snoring and how to avoid falling asleep and dropping your head on the shoulder of a complete stranger in the seat next to you.

In conclusion, you will learn the basic points of opera etiquette—never to applaud until the entire audience applauds (the aria may not be over even though it sounds like it is), how to shout the right phrases such as "brava!", and how to refer to certain operas by the "in" abbreviations ("Cav and Pag," "Barber," "Fig," "Carm," "Trov" and so on).

#19257—THE ITALIAN AND LATIN CROONERS: ARE THEY COMING BACK?
(Thurs., 9:00, $25)
John Mandarini

Mr. Mandarini, a veteran record producer and coauthor of *Vic Damone: An Unauthorized Biography*, contends that the style of the Republican administration, the growing conservatism of the middle class and the eagerness of the new college generation to assimilate into the establishment all point toward the revival of old-fashioned romantic crooners.

The day of the crooners may be upon us, the new descendants of Crosby, Sinatra, Tony Bennett and Perry Como are growing steadily in popularity and could sweep the country with their timeless, classic singing style. Mandarini will discuss the current status of such singers as Andy Russell, Alan Dale, Jerry Vale, Enzo Stuarti, Sergio Franchi, Jimmy Roselli, Dick Haymes and the rise of the new stars, Tony Romaine, Vito Arugula, Johnny Pasta, Frankie Pollo, Sergio Vitello, Andy Vongole and Russ Tortone.

#96311—BLIND, DEAF AND DUMB BLUES SINGERS
(Wed., 7:30, $25)
Barney Kitzel

The old saying "You've got to suffer if you want to sing the blues" has never found more truth than in the lives of the blind, deaf and dumb blues singers of the delta. Pioneers such as "Deaf Davy" Davidson, "Mute" Morris, and "Dumb Willie" Jefferson blazed a trail of musical expression that today surfaces in the rock stars of our generation—many of whom have to resort to powerful drugs to achieve the same handicaps.

Discovered near their small, rundown homes by sleazy promoters who recorded them, led them around the country performing in cheap dives, and often told them to "wait here on the corner" while they caught a good night's sleep in a hotel, the blind, deaf and dumb blues singers had *hard* lives. The irony of this history is that, with the rediscovery of this great art form, the few surviving singers today command six-figure salaries for a week in Vegas, and often spend entire years on the road in the Chitlin' Circuit.

In this course, Barney Kitzel tells you how these singers achieved their great success and, more importantly, how they mastered the techniques that made their art great—the moan, the eye-roll, and the syncopated foot-stomp. One remedial lesson will be provided in how to understand what the singers are saying, given their colorful use of the English language.

As a special treat, Mr. Kitzel has arranged for the appearances of two legendary blues singers, Maurice "Mudface" Williams and Larry "Loudmouth" Lincoln, who will perform for the class and then be led outside to "wait here on the corner" while their work is discussed.

#77659—MINERS' SONGS, CHANTS, HOLLERS
(Fri., 7:30, $25)
T. Walker Sibley

The songs and chants of the coal and iron miners have been difficult to collect for many years because of the dangerous working conditions. According to T. Walker Sibley, a sociologist and veteran collector of miners' songs, the miners had to sing in a very, very low voice—almost in a whisper. Had they sung at full volume, they would have started a cave-in. As a result, many of the early songs and chants were in the form of light hums, which also allowed the older miners, many of whom had lung and respiratory problems, to join in.

As working conditions improved, the miners began to take more chances and sing loudly. This was the beginning of the Golden Age of Miner's Songs (1955–1960), giving birth to such classics as Dusty Gray's *Rock's Around My Head, It's Dark Down Here, Tunnel's Closed* and *Help, I'm Trapped!* Unfortunately, the Golden Age came to an abrupt halt with the tragic cave-ins of the 60s.

Today, thanks to new rulings by the United Mine Workers' union, miners are singing in full voice once again, this time with the help of tiny microphones. They still whisper, but new electronic devices control the sound and volume for a safe level. A new generation of songs has been born, called "Rock 'n' Rock"—more sophisticated than the Golden Age music, fusing South African diamond mine chants with Russian slave camp songs.

Mr. Sibley will sing and play the latest miner's tapes, which will soon be released on Warner Brothers' records, entitled *Gray Lung Music*.

Related Courses in Music

Where to Find the Melodies in Modern Classical Music, #84421
The Influence of the Gregorian Chant on Phil Spector, #83315
The Life and Times of a Pip: An Analysis of Popular Song Through the Career of One of Gladys Knight's Backup Singers, #83333
Masterworks of Yiddish Opera, #88429

FILM

#36182–HOW TO BECOME A MOVIE PRODUCER
(Fri., 9:00, $30)
Marty Bernie

The old saying that anybody can be a movie producer is totally false and misleading. In today's highly competitive world of independent filmmaking the producer's job is extremely complex, requiring intense commitment and concentration.

This course offers a thorough grounding in the basics of how to become a successful film producer. You will learn how to acquire a "property" (script, play, novel, article, etc.) without actually paying the author; how to raise money and make the deal without committing any money of your own; how to acquire stars by playing one off the other; the Salkind Brothers method of getting two movies for the price of one (The Three and Four Musketeers); how to skim a huge, undetected sum out of the production budget; how to pad your expense account; how to use corporate funds for your personal needs; how to hide money from people who have a percentage of the profits; the Carlo Ponti Quadruple Entry Bookkeeping Technique; and most important, how to give the best oral sex to anyone important enough to help your career.

#66002–THIRTY-NINE EVENINGS WITH RINALDO NOVOLUCCI
(Dec. 1–Jan. 8, $150)
Rinaldo Novolucci

An unprecedented event in our film department—the chance to meet and hear Rinaldo Novolucci, one of the great directors of our time, in an informal class (enrollment is limited to twenty-four students).

Mr. Novolucci will discuss the development of his work from the early postwar period to his most recent film, *Crazy Monkeys*. He will lecture for thirty-nine consecutive days, showing excerpts from his films and answering any questions. He is also free for dinner and drinks after each lecture.

#37485–IS THERE A MOVIE IN IT?
How Film Scripts Are Derived from Anything
(Mon., 9:00, $40)
Victor Laszlo

There is an apocryphal story told of a meeting between three screenwriters engaged in creating a comedy. They were having great difficulty with a pivotal scene in the movie which required an ingenious piece of slapstick farce combined with some brilliantly witty dialogue. They worked on the scene for hours but could not come up with anything funny. The conference room looked like a hurricane had struck, with cigarette butts, half-eaten sandwiches, paper coffee cups and reams of discarded paper on the floor. The writers were exhausted. Finally the junior member of the group broke the silence and held up his watch to the others. He began to pull on the metal stretchband of his watch, flexing it back and forth. "Is there anything in this?" he asked, as he yanked and wiggled the watch band.

This story is the perfect metaphor for the state of the movie business today. No one knows where the next great commercial film idea will come from—it could been be inspired by a wristwatch stretchband.

This course will guide you to the most productive sources for movie ideas, the sources known only to the insiders of the film industry. You'll learn how to find these "bankable" ideas in the most unfamiliar places, and convert them into highly salable scripts—which is the only truly pragmatic, realistic approach to becoming a successful film writer.

The first section of the course explores the story possibilities in TV commercials, posters, songs, grafitti, matchbook covers, cookbooks, Annual Corporate Reports and the most important source, t-shirt slogans.

After a suitable subject is found, each student will be required to "develop" it, from a thought to a notion to an idea to a concept to a set of working notes, to a rough outline to a full outline to a treatment to a first-draft script to a second draft to a third draft to a "polish" to a final draft to a shooting script to a rejection to a "turnaround" (sale to another studio) to a final rejection.

#00176–HOW TO BREAK INTO A MOVIE
(Thurs., 7:30, $15)
Jay Bumbardo

Many of today's hottest actors and actresses were "discovered" on the locations of actual film shootings. They accomplished this feat by "breaking into" a movie that was being shot, and by their actions and improvisations on the set. The sheer nerve and daring of interrupting a movie costing as much as $50 million creates an indelible impression on a director and producer always on the lookout for new, exciting talent.

This course will show you how to sneak onto the set of any film, whether it's an outdoor or indoor set, how to fool

OVER-EXTENSION UNIVERSITY BULLETIN

security police, how to walk right into the middle of a scene, how to hang around the set and become friendly with the principals, how to become a "gofer," an errand boy, and most important, how to land a part in the movie.

#00177—HOW TO BREAK INTO A MOVIE HOUSE
(Thurs, 9:00, $45)
Jay Bumbardo

For those whose love of film is not as intense we also offer a course in how to break into a movie theater without paying. The emphasis will be on rear entry, such as finding the little-known fire exits and slipping in with a flashlight (holding a flashlight gives you the appearance of an usher). Other techniques include dressing as a service man (an air-conditioner repairman, a popcorn supplier, an electrician, a plumber for the bathrooms, a candy supplier). Once you have made your "repair" or checked the inventory of chocolate mints and popcorn, you can simply disappear into the darkness of the theater and watch the movie.

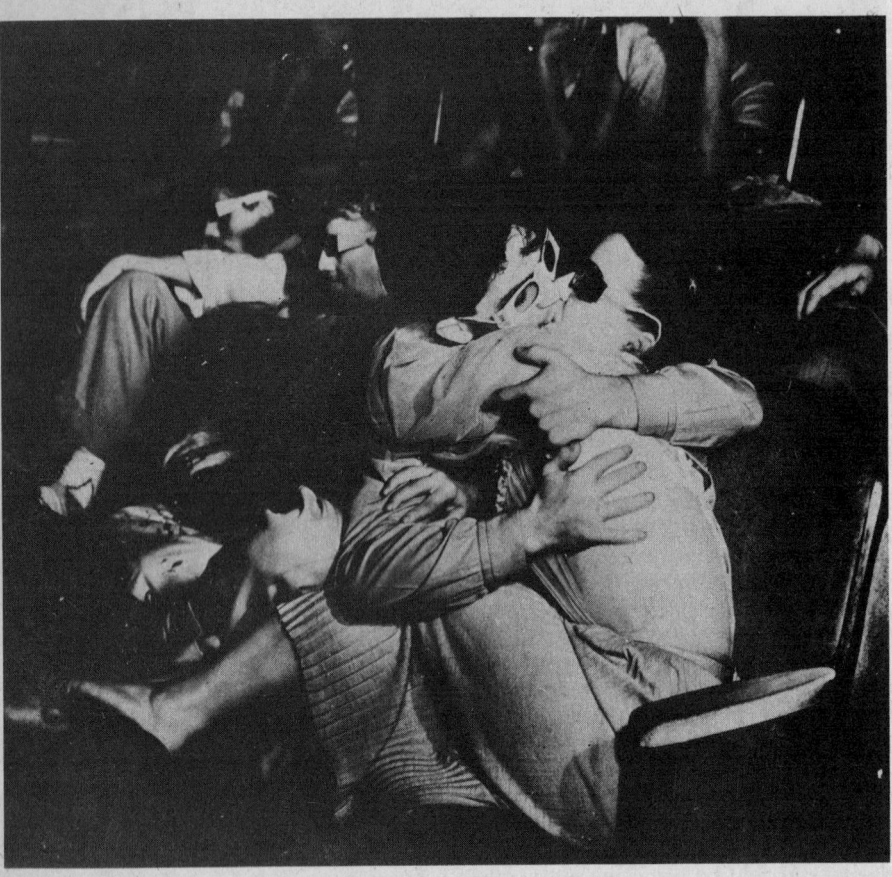

#58376—TEN CINEMATIC EVENINGS
Rare, offbeat films, many never seen before
Discussion sessions will follow. Surprise guests whenever possible.
(Fri. eves., $3)
Egbert St. John

Nov. 2—	The Lesser Known Films of Chad Everett
Nov. 9—	Screwball Tragedies of the 30s
Nov. 16—	Latvian Animated Shorts: 1949–1981
Nov. 23—	Fat on Film: Highlights of the Works of Orson Welles, Victor Buono, Peter Ustinov, Burl Ives and Sidney Greenstreet
Nov. 30—	Belgian World War I Propoganda Films
Dec. 7—	Cantinflas and the Art of Suspense
Dec. 14—	Moslem Musicals
Dec. 21—	The Science Fiction Films of Zsa Zsa Gabor
Dec. 28—	The Bedroom Comedies of Bresson and Dryer
Jan 4—	*Josephine,* the Sequel to Abel Gance's *Napoleon*

#40682—SCREWBALL TRAGEDIES OF THE 40s
A Film Survey
(Wed., 7:30, $40)
Stanley Vermin

Somewhere between *Film Noir* and *Film Blanc* is the screwball tragedy of *Film Gris* ("Grey film"), an odd genre that is a mixture of the lighthearted *Blanc* and the grim, tragic *Noir* schools.

Many of the most brilliant directors of the 30s and 40s felt a need to show more of the tragic side of life, the reality behind the usual glossy Hollywood version. Occasionally, a well-established director would be allowed by the studio moguls to do a film of this sort, but only if he also injected plenty of zany comedy and optimism into the picture, no matter how contradictory the results. The tragic scenes could suddenly shift into wacky, lovable comedy. The screwball scenes would end in grim tragedy. This often left both the directors and the audiences confused. Nevertheless, a very small, moderately enthusiastic cult developed for this group of films though they had only a brief life span.

In 1962, the French film magazine *Cashiers du Cinéma* devoted an entire issue to this forgotten genre, with profound tributes by Jean-Luc Godard, François Truffaut, Eric Rohmer and André Bazin. They christened it *Film Gris*, somewhere between dark and light. Godard described Samuel Fuller's *Crazy Mixed Up Kid,* "the greatest movie ever made . . . one of the greatest works of art ever made." Bazin was delirious over the performance of Dale Robertson in Nick Ray's *They Drink by Night*, and it was rumored that he was reduced to babble and baby talk when praising Robertson to friends in cafes. Even the more level-headed, less dogmatic Truffaut wrote of Stanley Donen's *Not-So-Funny Face*, . . . "it is somewhere between farce, slapstick, musical, high drama, melodrama and cartoon, and this is as it should be. *Not-So Funny Face* is pure cinema, the cinema of confusion and doubt and inconsistency. It is a work of genius that can never be duplicated."

Stanley Vermin has culled the archives of RKO, Universal, Columbia and 20th Century Fox to find some of the more offbeat and adventurous samples of this odd hybrid of the cinema. Each film will be prefaced by a brief discussion and many surprise guests will appear.

(Nov. 1) *Cocktails at Sing Sing*—
Directed by Samuel Fuller

Fuller's story involves identical twins, one a madcap playboy, the other a convicted murderer, along with a dizzy female ornithologist, a camel that sings and a baby dolphin, the first time a dolphin

40   *The Performing Arts*

was ever used in a serious film role (long before Flipper). The plot is shaky, but as usual with Fuller, the action is grim and graphic. Best scene: the playboy, mistaken for his brother, is led to the electric chair, screaming and crying, while the escaped criminal brother is sipping a martini at the Ritz with his singing camel. With Guy Madison in a dual role. Also starring Ruth Roman and Virginia Mayo.

(Nov. 8) *Animal, Vegetable or Mineral?*—Directed by Nicholas Ray

Completed After *Rebel Without a Cause*, but never shown publicly in the U.S. (it was a big hit in Europe), Nick Ray's *Animal, Vegetable or Mineral?* is typical of his obsession with prominent social themes. In this case it's euthenasia, and only Ray would have the audacity to turn this subject into a screwball tragedy. Gloria Grahame plays the "vegetable" in this film, a precursor of Karen Ann Quinlan, with Glenn Ford as her tormented husband who can't afford the enormous medical costs of keeping her alive and has to take three jobs to pay the expenses. The ending is Ray at his bravura best. Ford is about to die of sheer exhaustion and finally decides to kill himself and his wife with a pair of bullets. Suddenly, by a miracle, Grahame stirs, awakens and shoots Ford first with a gun she had hidden under her pillow.

(Nov. 15) *Fools Die First*—Directed by Fritz Lang

A college professor is mistaken for an internationally prominent scientist who has discovered a serum that will cure flatulence. The evil underworld mastermind, Felix Von Krell (yet another version of Lang's Dr. Mabuse) kidnaps the unwitting Professor Schlump (Eddie Bracken) as he tries to take world control of this new miracle drug. Commenting on the drug, Von Krell says, "If Hitler had this serum he would have never lost the war."

Shot in 1952, on a campus in West Germany, it combines Lang's usual elements of greed, blackmail, lurid sex and murder with daffy "mad scientist" routines and a bunch of young German college fraternity members, who, among other things, like to fight duels with huge liverwursts. There are even some college musical numbers and student drinking songs sprinkled among the murders and sadistic torture scenes. Also starring Robert Stack, Lizabeth Scott and Dean Stockwell.

(Nov. 22) *Fort Patched-Up*—Directed by John Ford

Our greatest cinematic storyteller and poet of the old west must have had something else in mind when he directed this film, or perhaps the studios went over-

board in interfering with his artistic vision. The results were mixed, to say the least. This was not only a screwball tragedy, but a period screwball tragedy, set in Ford's familiar western territory of the 1860s. The studio could not get Ford's regular stock group (Henry Fonda, Jimmy Stewart, or even Ward Bond, Harry Carey and Woody Strode) to appear in this odd genre so he had to use two unfamiliar leads, Richard Egan and Rory Calhoun, two rather stiff tragi-comic farceurs. The story constantly shifts scenes from a remote outpost in the far west to Washington, D.C, where Rory Calhoun, a crazed southern dirt farmer is trying to assassinate President Grant, (nicely underacted by Cesar Romero). Ford uses the Indians primarily as the screwballs, a bunch of savages who can't stage an ambush, rape, loot or kill their white enemies without screwing up the works. Somehow, Calhoun is enlisted on their side and Richard Egan, a U.S. Cavalry marshall, is their adversary. Everyone dies in the end, which is true to the screwball tragedy tradition, and Ford does it with even more alacrity and dispatch than usual in a brilliant effort to rid himself of this strange little saga. When asked about *Fort Patched-Up*, the gruff old master said, "All I wanted to do was wash up, get my money and go home."

(Nov. 29) *Citizen Kung*—Directed by Orson Welles

Welles's idea was no less than doing a screwball tragedy version of his own *Citizen Kane*. His first mistake was to transfer the setting of his story to a small village in China. The problem was compounded when it was discovered that it was terribly difficult to find anyone to play real Chinese except Keye Luke and a few leftovers from World War II films. Welles casted himself as the idiot Emperor Wing Wang and Joseph Cotten as Kung, a crippled newsboy who wants to become a publishing tycoon in Shanghai.

Stock racist jokes alternate with horrifying scenes of Tong wars and the looting, pillaging and raping of small towns by the warlords. The only consolation in this film for Welles was his chance to use real Chinese food for his banquet scenes and food fights (he was already in his extra-plump stage). About halfway through the movie, Welles was fired for one of his celebrated excesses—he spent over $800,000 on the catering for one Chinese tea lunch scene alone. Eventually, Frank Tashlin replaced Welles and re-shot the second half of the film with Jayne Mansfield and Johnny Weissmuller, which gave it a schizoid, slapstick quality even Welles couldn't duplicate.

Related Courses in Film

A History of Deservedly Forgotten Movies, #86753

Classics of Limited Animation Cartoons, #83215

The Norwegian Documentary, #81459

The Red-Head in Film, #88467

The New Cinema of Luxembourg, #79395

The Sit-Com as Absurdist Art, #79386

The 10 Greatest Sex Loops Ever Made, #78374

How to Fine Tune an Old TV Set, #76543

THEATRE

#29385—SVEVO LIVING PUPPET THEATER OF LATVIA WORKSHOP
(Mon., 9:00, $40)
Svevo Living Puppet Theater

"All people are puppets. Those few who are in power pull the strings." This was the guiding theme of Ladniak Svevo when he formed his Living Puppet Theater in Latvia in 1932. Svevo, a dedicated anarchist and an amateur weight lifter, believed that conventional acting methods could not adequately convey the injustices and inequities that had befallen modern man.

Svevo's Latvia had long been a stronghold of traditional puppet theater. Every Latvian child grows up with hand puppets and little puppet theaters. It is not uncommon for Latvians to take a set of puppet characters with them wherever they go, in their shoulder and handbags, so they can practice their routines anywhere.

Latvians like to assume the identities of the puppet characters they create and communicate with each other through these characters, instead of direct talk. This is their time-honored way of escaping the dreariness and boredom of their everyday lives.

Svevo took the common artifact of Latvian life and transformed it into a Brechtian icon—the puppet as Man. Instead of the tiny puppet theater operated by humans manipulating puppets on strings, he made his actors into puppets and had his puppeteers manipulate them. Obviously this requires very talented, versatile actors and very strong puppeteers. This is where Svevo's weight lifting talents were helpful. At first he had to figure out how to disguise the fact that his actors were live puppets. Normally, the wires controlling puppets are invisible, but in 1932 there were no invisible wires made in Latvia. Svevo hit on the idea of attaching stout ropes to his actors and painting the ropes in the same color as his scenic backdrop so they would blend in and go unnoticed. This was successsful, but there was the problem of how to manipulate human puppets for up to three or four hours without exhausting the stamina of the puppeteers, especially when there was very little food in Latvia in the 30s.

Needless to say, Svevo never solved this thorny problem and his Living Puppet Theater was forced to go underground during the Stalinist era and World War II. Today his son Urbniak is continuing his father's revered tradition with modern technology and conditioning methods to

make things much easier. Instead of rope to control the actor-puppets, there is invisible nylon wire—100,000 times stronger than conventional hemp. Operating the actors are professional weight lifters who do not have to utter a word. This leaves actors free to simply act and dangle in front of the audience.

Urbniak Svevo will instruct you in how to build your own living puppet theater, how to condition and train yourself to become a Svevo-style puppeteer and how to act like a puppet for the actual performances. The repertoire of the Svevo theater consists of traditional Latvian folk tales, classics of the theater in the nineteenth and twentieth centuries and the most avant-garde plays of today.

#39872—THIRD WORLD STAND-UP COMEDY WORKSHOP
(Wed., 9:00, $25)
Barry Bugman

The New Wave of future comedy may very well come from the exciting, provocative performers developing their art and craft in the Third World countries of Africa, Asia and the Arab states. Many of these new comedians are working in entirely different forms and techniques, completely removed from their Western counterparts. Some are still crude and unformed, relying on simple native rituals and customs, others are remarkably sophisticated and profound, offering social statements recalling the best work of Lenny Bruce and Richard Pryor.

Most Africans have a robust, hearty sense of humor. However, the basic forms of Western stand-up comedy, the joke and the monologue, are virtually unknown. An African would find our funny stories totally incomprehensible even when perfectly translated. Instead of telling jokes to get laughs, the Africans like to make believe they are eating themselves. They bite and chew on their bodies and make various sounds and cries that are truly comical in nature. Nothing can bring an African to tears of laughter faster than a traditional *M'wonga* routine, which roughly translates as a "toe biting bit." Other forms of *M'wonga* include elbow biting and eating your nose. Although he is now in his seventies, the Nigerian comedian Togo is still considered the greatest *M'wonga* artist in African history, and we are fortunate to have a rare collection of Togo's performances on film, compiled by Barry Bugman, a prominent stand-up comedian and an expert in African humor. Mr. Bugman will analyze and interpret Togo's most famous routines, "Eat Your Entire Body" and "Bite Your Neck."

The Oriental comedians coming out of mainland China, Taiwan, Vietnam, Korea and Japan have a more varied style and repertoire, ranging from the Chinese who can do a non-stop monologue for thirty minutes or more without catching a breath to the "minimalist" style of Japanese Rice Comedy in which the comedian pretends he is a single grain of rice and attempts to make his condition a humorous one. Barry Bugman interprets Oriental comedy as "a very conscious attempt to create a non-funny form, something very serious or incredibly boring and mundane, and then trying to convert it into a funny piece of business, like the 'Grain of Rice Bit.' You never consciously start as a normal comedian, you sort of back into the bit."

Koreans lay great emphasis on garlic in their comedy. Garlic is a staple in their cooking, along with hot peppers, and somehow garlic became a funny symbol. Calling someone a clove of garlic in Korea will get a big laugh. Many of the Korean comedians get even more mileage out of this by dressing as garlic cloves. Each comedian has his own odd and funny costume and does his numbers differently, though all the stories have the same punch line, something about garlic. The most difficult Oriental comedy to master and one that is rarely seen in this country is from the Philippines. The Filipino comedian selects someone from the audience and slaps his face very hard. This usually provokes a violent fight. At this point the comedian tries to escape from the outraged, publicly insulted victim and tries to amuse and placate him with stories, songs and bird imitations.

All Moslem comedians are female impersonators. This is the tradition and cannot be changed. It is fairly easy for a Moslem to become a "female." All he needs is a veil, a little eye flutter technique and perhaps a falsetto voice. Mr. Bugman feels that this form comes from the fact that most Moslem countries treat women as second class citizens, objects of ridicule and satire. The routines are more like character studies—a woman getting robbed and beaten, a woman getting raped, a woman falling into the mud, a woman getting urinated on by a monkey and so on. They all bring howls of laughter from the Moslem audiences.

Aside from Barry Bugman, there will be guest lecturers and comedians directly from the Third World. Our final session will be a visit to Jomo's, the first African comedy improvisation club in the city.

#87321–ACTING YOUR WAY OUT OF A PAPER BAG
(Thurs., 9:00, $35)
Ivor Boneyard

Everyone at one time or another has wanted to act, to bask in the limelight, to "ham it up" and milk the applause of a cheering audience. Unfortunately, very few of us are blessed with the God-given talent necessary to make it to the top or even to the middle and bottom rungs of the ladder. But this doesn't mean that the serious amateur, or even the ordinary well-meaning dabbler cannot enjoy some of the same rewards as the professionals.

Even if you've never acted before, Ivor Boneyard, Director of the Mighty Thespians of Thor Playhouse, will show you how to do it with his patented "Poof, You're an Actor" method. "Even the shyest, worst actors in the world can do it," says Boneyard. "Especially the ones who say they can't act their way out of a paper bag. I say they can. And I show them how."

The main section of the course will demonstrate how to act your way out of a paper bag, a large, life-size paper bag which is placed over your body.

Intermediate and advanced classes will study how to act your way out of telephone booths, closets, elevators and small cars.

#13254–MICHAEL MARCEAU'S WORD MIME WORKSHOP
(Fri., 7:30, $30, Beg.; Fri., 9:00, $35, adv.)
Michael Marceau and his Word Mime Troupe

(For one semester only, Michael Marceau and his full cast of word mimes will teach a basic and an advanced course. Space will be limited. Please register early.)

Michael Marceau (no relation to Marcel) is not nearly as well known, but he, too, offers a highly original mime technique, the only kind in the world that also uses spoken words. His critics have been outspoken in insisting that his technique is not pure mime, that he tells the audience too much, giving them long descriptions of what he is about to do, or punctuating a routine with spoken jokes, dialogue or song. "Monsieur Michael," as he is called, dismisses his critics as ultra-conservative guardians of a near obsolete art. "Pure mime is boring. I bring new life to a moribund form," he says.

There can be no question that Michael's mime is much easier to understand than the old form popularized by Marcel Marceau. When Michael Marceau does his famous "man riding up an escalator," he tells you out loud exactly how far up he's progressed, what department of the store he is in, what the other people look like, and so on. His troupe communicates with each other through the spoken word as well as the gesture, with quick bursts of dialogue as well as detailed descriptions of their silent movements.

The basic course covers M. Michael's broader techniques. The advanced course will concentrate on the more word-oriented techniques, culminating in his famous word mime version of *Hamlet*.

DANCE

#81124—HASIDIC BALLROOM DANCING
(Tues., 7:30, $25)
Professor Morris Bluestein

Hasidic ballroom dancing had its origins in the mid-eighteenth century in eastern Europe in the *shtetls*, the small towns that had a large Jewish ghetto population. The Hasidim were an orthodox sect that believed in achieving grace through learning, singing and dancing their religious hymns. Dancing was especially important, but the early styles were exclusively communal and folkish. And always, they were segregated. Men were forbidden to dance with women.

The first Hasidic ballroom step is credited to Meyer Ben Ernst, the son of the legendary Ernst Lubitcher Rabbi of Russia. In the middle of a folk dance, out of sheer boredom, Meyer seized his closest partner and broke away from the group, whirling the other in a waltz-like frenzy. He was banished from the congregation along with his partner. Rather than accepting the humiliation and repenting, Meyer and his partner became a dance team, making up their own steps and touring the Russian shtetl circuit where they were known as the "Steppe Brothers."

Needless to say, the Steppe Brothers were outlawed by the bluenosed rabbinical elders and had to perform in secret, in midnight shows, to audiences that heard of their notoriety through word of mouth. After only six months of touring they were stoned to death in Kiev by a band of irate Orthodox rabbis, but not before their magical dance steps were memorized by thousands of underground fans and groupies.

Morris Bluestein, a professor of Hasidic Studies at Yeshiva Tech, has written the definitive work on the subject, *Dance, Jew, Dance!*

He divides the history of the Hasidic Dance into three phases—Early, Middle and Later. The Early Phase was dominated by the Steppe Brothers and their legacy. The dances were either very, very fast—a whirling dervish type—or very slow and stately, using a step remarkably similar to the Tango. All dancing was done by men only.

The Middle Phase, which began in the late nineteenth century features dances such as the *Chachka*, a very elaborate, intricate step that was inspired by the sacred book of the mystics, the Kabbala, and is based on a series of complex numerological formulas and phases of the moon.

The Late Phase, which takes us to the present, is far more liberated and is currently popular with the younger Hasidic set, who like to refer to their dances as "Saturday Night Fever", that time right after the Sabbath laws have been lifted when everyone can lead a more normal life, dance and "freak out." It is rumored that many of them are dancing with female partners.

● BONUS GIFT OFFER ●

Bring in a new student and get a free gift!
For one student you get a free Foster-Trilex Toaster!
Bring in two students and receive a free Saywa Cassette Recorder!
Three students wins you a Mamyo Radio-Cassette-Camera combination!
Four students gives you a Shubita 14" black- and-white TV portable!
For five new students you get a Yamaka Complete Home Stereo Entertainment Center and a weekend for two in San Juan, Puerto Rico!

#91473—PAUL TRINKLER INSECT BALLET WORKSHOP
(Fri., 7:30, $25)
Paul Trinkler

The modern dance company of Paul Trinkler offers a workshop and seminar advancing Mr. Trinkler's unusual theories and choreography based on the movements and behavior of the insect kingdom.

For many years Paul Trinkler studied the dance styles of insects with his good friend and collaborator, the noted entomologist Otto Boorvis. Together they evolved the now familiar Trinkler ballet style which adapts insect behavior patterns into full-length ballets to be danced by humans.

Mr. Trinkler will discuss the creation of his most famous works, "Mating Dance," "Survival of the Fittest," "Flies in My Soup," "The Flyswatter Suite," and "Sleeping Beetle." The final lecture will deal with the psycho-cultural importance of insect behavior in relationship to the dance. There will also be a chance to wear many of Mr. Trinkler's fabulous insect costumes.

OVER-EXTENSION UNIVERSITY BULLETIN

TELEVISION

#57354—LITTLE-KNOWN TV SHOWS OF THE 50s
A Nostalgic Survey
(Mon., 7:30, $25)
Leonard Haymish

Not the hit shows, not even the also-rans, but the outright failures—the shows that were aired once and were abruptly cancelled! Upon re-examination, TV critic Leonard Haymish finds that many of these shows have an odd period charm and a peculiarly adventurous approach that makes them extremely likable today. Mr. Haymish will offer thoughtful, sympathetic analyses of the shows with kinescopes of actual episodes whenever possible.

(Oct. 24)
Car Parking Derby
The world's fastest car parking attendants compete in the gigantic San Fernando Shopping Mall while a drama of young love unfolds between an assistant manager and a checkout girl in the Mall's big supermarket. A daring attempt to combine a game show with a soap opera. Warren Tobago is your host.

(Oct. 31)
Leonardo Rembrandt, P.D.
Leonardo Rembrandt is a young police sketch artist whose composite portraits are used to catch dangerous wanted criminals. Rembrandt struggles in vain to introduce a more "free" abstract style to his portraits in his never-ending battles with the crusty police chief, O'Goyahan. With George Biblo and Stephen Thorne.

(Nov. 7)
Solomon's Six Guns
A band of cowboys enter a time machine and find themselves back in the reign of King Solomon. Wacky misadventures ensue as they team up with the wise old King and his thousand wives to fight the hostile Arab tribes. Stars Chuck Manners, Garth McCord, Nancy Loam.

(Nov. 14)
Hair Today, Gone Tomorrow
Members of the studio audience get their hair cut and styled by a leading Hollywood hairdresser, plus the Celebrity Haircut and Manicure of the week. Betty Muggles and Johnny Sparks are your co-hosts.

(Nov. 21)
Steve Strong, Warehouseman
Steve Strong is a troubleshooter for Acme Warehouses, a nationwide chain that specializes in storing priceless works of art. With Don Boff as Steve and Ben Secundo as his sidekick, Ben.

(Nov. 28)
Charley's Ants
Charley Jones is the owner of a small mail-order ant farm business that he runs with his wife Minna, his son Midge and his daughter Bobo. But the ants seem to have

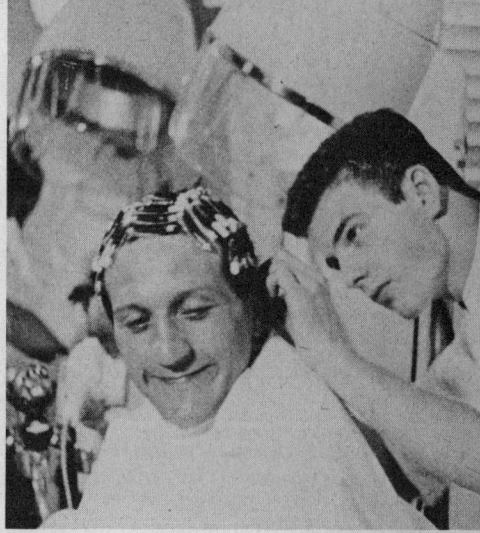

minds of their own and drive Charley crazy. Stars Walter Pudge and Gloria Novis.

(Dec. 5)
Head of the Family
Johnny Sparks plays a young newlywed who goes prematurely bald and has to learn how to live with it. Sally Croomes plays his lovable but unsympathetic wife. (Both *Head of the Family* and *Hair Today, Gone Tomorrow* were developed by Garry Pap, who used Johnny Sparks as his star when *Hair Today* was cancelled.)

(Dec. 12)
Zoo Police
Greg Masters stars as Sargeant Speed Mulvaney, head of safety and security at the San Diego Zoo. Stories of adventure, suspense and warm human interest. Also starring Leslie Corday and Selma, the talking goose.

(Dec. 19)
Mr. Nobody
A delightful children's show starring Miles Filibuster as Mr. Nobody, the man no one knows or remembers, with his little family of non-entities, Billy Boring, the Invisible Girl and Kinko, the paralyzed clown.

(Dec. 26)
Lloyd's of Dublin
Aloysius Xavier Lloyd starts a small insurance company in Dublin with the goal of becoming another Lloyd's of London. Lots of obstacles, pitfalls and goofy mishaps make him wonder if he should try another business. Starring Hugh Bolster and Cindy Proust.

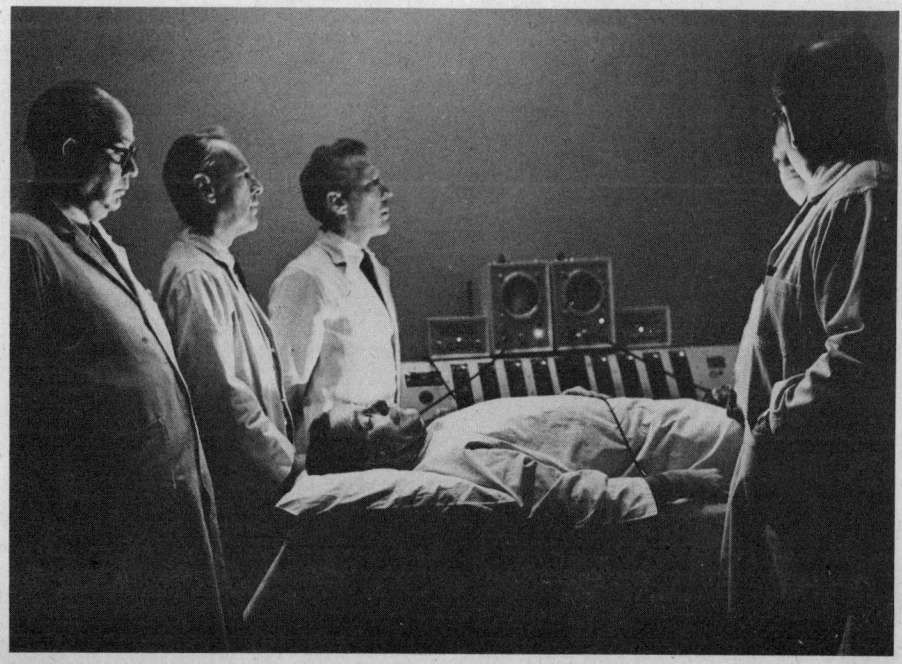

The Performing Arts 45

SCIENCE

#92589–THE REAL LIFE OF THE SOLAR SYSTEM
(Thurs., 7:30, $30)
Dr. Marvin J. Nickstein

Because of the many government restrictions on releasing secret, classified data, most of us will never come remotely close to getting the truth about the real life on other planets and galaxies. Marvin J. Nickstein, a former administrator of the NASA program and an expert in interplanetary research, has written a brilliant new book on life in the solar system for the layman called *Who's Who and What's What In Outer Space*. This course is adapted from his book, with many new revelations and discoveries.

Mr. Nickstein will describe in great detail, with actual photos taken from NASA files, such phenomena as the Potato People of Venus, the undersea plants of Neptune that can engage in real sexual intercourse and a shrub on Mars from which one small leaf contains enough nutrition to keep the entire population of Yugoslavia healthy for the next twenty-five years. You'll learn about the gigantic oil deposits, still untouched, on Uranus, the riddle of the microwave oven found on Saturn and where many other "odd little people" dwell.

Because of the highly secretive and controversial nature of the subject, Mr. Nickstein (actually an alias) will be visible but will speak from behind an opaque screen. Prospective students will be required to show that they and their friends and familes do not have any connections with government or military agencies.

#38754–A NEW LOOK AT ALCHEMY
(Tues., 7:30, $25)
Louis Pintchek

Once the most respected of all sciences, then scorned and ridiculed for centuries, alchemy, the chemistry of creating gold out of baser metals, is undergoing a new revival for both scientific and monetary reasons.

Certain scientists in both the United States and Russia are pursuing a new alchemical theory that attempts to transmute gold out of nonmetallic materials instead of metal, with considerable progress reported. Most of the experiments have been highly secret, but Mr. Pintchek has obtained some pictures taken with hidden cameras at one of the alchemy laboratories in Texas which show small amounts of a gold-like metal being produced out of bean curd cakes after being subjected to nuclear and laser bombardment.

With the photographs and other data gleaned from scientific journals and confidential government reports, Mr. Pintchek has put together a fascinating study of this bold new attempt to conquer one of mankind's most complex chemical problems.

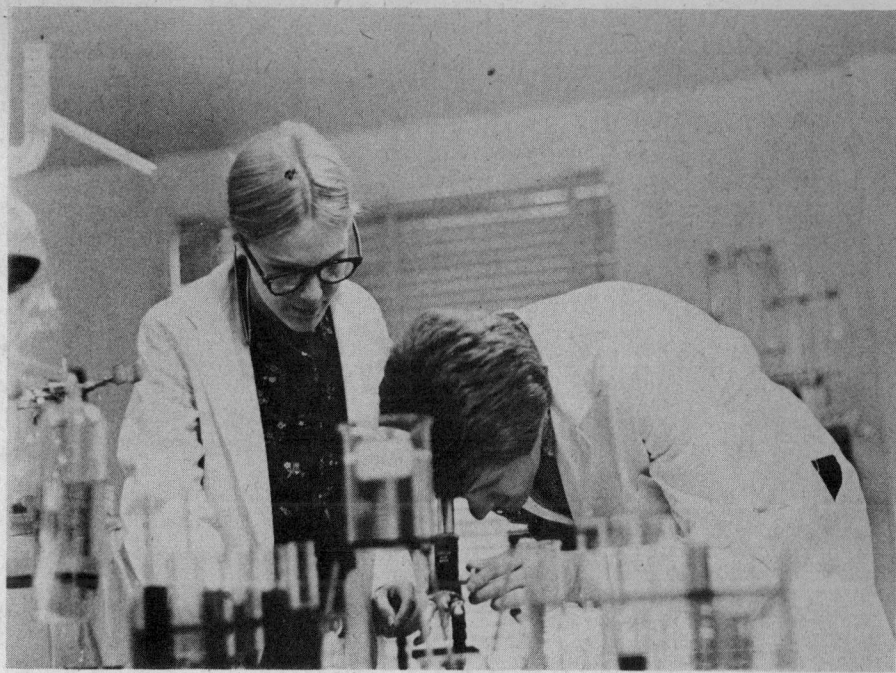

#87634–NEW FRONTIERS OF SCIENCE
A Survey of the Newest Scientific Disciplines
(Wed., 7:30, $40)
Louis Pintchek

The world of science moves at such a dizzying pace that it seems like a new highway or by-way of learning opens almost every day challenging and questioning the old theories. This course will offer an outline of some of the daring new scientific theories, explaining them in layman's terms, with the emphasis on how they relate to the real world around us and to survival of mankind in the twenty-first century.

Mr. Pintchek will discuss Thermogenetics, the theory of chromosome stress techniques in wind tunnels; Hormonal Physics, an explanation of certain physical laws of our pituitary glands; Astrobiology, the study of human life outside the solar system; and the "White Holes" of Venus. There will be a special attempt to explain the inter-relationships of these disciplines which so far, have not been successful, but Mr. Pintchek promises that he will try his best.

#15304–THE SECRET LIFE OF UNBORN PLANTS
(Tues., 9:00, $25)
Lanislaw Kelb

A new branch of botanical research is the theory that many plants have a fully developed "life" before they are actually born.

The pioneering work of Harkavy and Broode at London University has already proven that germinating plants have well-formed ideas, habits and growth patterns. In their famous study of the hardy perennials at Kew Gardens, Harkavy and Broode examined 250 plant buds and predicted which would grow up healthy and which wouldn't. Their accuracy rate was a remarkable 94 percent. It would have been 97 percent if the accidental plant deaths were considered.

Lanislaw Kelb is a disciple of Harkavy and Broode and will present an easy to follow introduction of their highly complex work. Using both botanical evidence, mathematical logic and computerized information we will be able to see how an unborn plant "feels" and "thinks," how it reacts to the environment, how certain sounds can influence its future size and shape and a confirmation of the fact that even *unborn* plants react positively and negatively to certain types of music.

Students will be required to bring in their own plant buds for analysis and growth predictions.

#19320–INTRODUCTION TO MATHEMATICS
(Thurs., 7:30, $15)
Leonard Spicke

This is an introductory course to acquaint students with the basic principles of arithmetic, algebra and geometry. It will also introduce some important concepts in mathematical logic and number theory and explain the techniques of problem solving using the basic mathematical syntax.

#19321–INTRODUCTION TO MATHEMATICS
(Thurs., 9:00, $17.50)
Leonard Spicke

This is a follow-up and reiteration of Introduction to Mathematics if you did not comprehend it initially. It will repeat the same material as the first course—basic principles of arithmetic, algebra and geometry. It will again cover important concepts in mathematical logic and number theory and explain the techniques of problems solving using basic mathematical syntax.

#19322–INTRODUCTION TO MATHEMATICS
(Fri., 7:30, $20)
Leonard Spicke

This is a refresher course containing the same material as the two previously listed courses, for those who are still not sure they've grasped all the basic principles. Special attention will be paid to arithmetic, algebra and geometry. We will also cover important concepts in mathematical logic and number theory and explain the techniques of problem solving using basic mathematical syntax.

HUMANITIES

LITERATURE

#88932–KAFKA'S PROBLEM WITH THE PRAGUE TELEPHONE COMPANY
(Wed., 9:00, $30)
Boric Abrahams

Just when we thought there could be no other work on Franz Kafka, we find yet another brilliant fragment unearthed by the German scholar and biographer Bruno Von Mieskeit, *The Transcribed Conversations of Franz Kafka with the Prague Phone Company*.

We are fortunate to have Boric Abrahams, the translator of Von Mieskeit's work, and a noted Kafka scholar in his own right, to discuss the book.

In 1922, Kafka summoned up enough courage to have his own telephone installed, though he secretly dreaded using the instrument, much preferring to write people, even if he were promising to meet them on the same day for coffee or lunch. Many of his friends and relatives had a telephone and constantly urged him to have one of his own. After suffering intense headaches and gastrointestinal illnesses resisting the pressures of his peers, he finally succumbed and ordered a telephone from the Prague Telephonic Gesellschaft on April 2, 1922. From that point on, his life turned into a nightmare.

It took Kafka over seven months to make his first phone call. When he picked up the phone to dial he relates that "my eyes could not fathom the numbers on the dialing mechanism. I had a horrible mental block. I could not remember who I was supposed to call or what the numbers were. I felt dizzy, weak, afraid that this ugly black instrument would somehow destroy me."

But a strange thing happened when Kafka finally held the phone to his ear. He heard voices. Not ghostly spirits, but real human voices, voices speaking to each other in a most profoundly personal and revealing manner. He was horrified but oddly fascinated. Every day he would pick up the phone and more often than not, hear these voices, as if an entire city's life had been laid bare for him. He was too terrified to ever interrupt any of the conversations, but he had the curiosity and patience (and the shorthand skill) to transcribe the voices to paper. He would then agonize over so and so's horrible venereal disease problem, so and so's affair with a Russian count, a quarrel between husband and mistress, a pathetic plea for money. What Kafka never knew was that his phone was hooked up to a party line.

Kafka was at a loss over how to react to the hundreds of tragic problems, pathetic affairs and morbid fears he overheard. Finally, he began writing letters to the telephone company about the odd behavior of his phone. But each time a repairman examined it, he found nothing wrong.

Kafka stopped listening to the phone conversations, but by now the voices tormented him and would not let him do his normal work or sleep at night. He would remember every voice, every nuance, every inflection. He was going mad. One day his sister visited and found him with his head buried in a large bowl of *schlag* (whipped cream). He was mute with despair and madness. She took him away to a nearby spa for rest and recuperation.

When Kafka recovered and returned home he discovered his phone was gone. It had been disengaged by the company, he learned, because he had not paid his bill for three months. A summons was issued for him to appear in civil court, which further traumatized him, but after paying the bill he began to forget the voices and his life soon became relatively normal.

The conversations have been edited by Von Mieskeit and organized into a coherent pattern. Along with Kafka's own marginal notes and entries, *The Prague Phone Company* again takes us into the eerie, neurotic, alienated and brilliantly insightful world of this major writer.

#73681—GOOD BOOKS AND GOOD READS: A Study In High Contrast
(Tues., 9:00, $30)
Hugh Tungwell

Mr. Tungwell, author of *How to Read a Read*, explains why the standard concepts of "Art and Literature" are wrongly opposed to the concepts of "Schlock and Crap." In explaining his radical theories, he absolves students of guilt for enjoying such contemporary works as Sidney Sheldon's "Bloodline" while at the same time questioning the intellectual pretension that would lead them to antique quirks such as "The Scarlet Letter."

The course begins by explaining the essential elements of the Good Read—

characters, plot, a nice cover, clear type, wide margins, and frequent scenes in limousines and penthouses. Mr. Tungwell then challenges the critics of the Good Read, who call these books "irrelevant and ultimately forgettable." "Certainly you can forget a lot that is in these books," Tungwell counters, "but then you can fill in your own facts—this allows the good read to speak to many people, on many different levels."

Finally, Tungwell contrasts the good read with the good book using the "accepted" standards of literature. He finds that the contemporary novel compares favorably with the "classics"—witness the brilliant grasp of nuance and social strata in *Remembrance of Things Past* and *Scruples*; the mastery of a special world and the spellbinding power of *Moby Dick* and *Cujo*; the haunting luminosity of *Les Misérables* and *Sweet Savage Love*.

"Genius is overused as a concept," Tungwell concludes, "so let's drop it and give some guys a break."

#00198—THE SEPHARDIC HERMAPHRODITE: Grotesques in Latin American Literature
(Thurs., 9:00, $25)
Manuel Buick

Hermaphrodite dwarfs, single breasted monkey women, giant nubians with heads of condors, half-men half-turkeys, children with enormous genitalia—these and much more are the basic ingredients for many of the most important writers in Latin America today. Are they symbolic characters or do they really exist? Are they the products of the novelists' steaming imagination or do they come from the steaming jungles of the Amazon and the terrifying interiors of the Andes? We do not know for sure, but they do provide some of the most exciting new literary works of the last decade.

This course will study the works of Jorge Pontual (*Rotten Limes, One Thousand Years of Indecision*), Pedro Malan (*Santa Catarina, The Last Days of Ziraldo the Great,*) Ivan Lessa (*The Spider's Kiss*), and Tarik de Sauza (*Little Black Samba, Give Me the Head of Jayne Mansfield*).

#93002—F. SCOTT FITZGERALD AND THE BEATLES: A Study in Counterpoint
(Tues., 7:30, $20)
George Lunger

When F. Scott Fitzgerald and the Beatles were at the peaks of their respective careers they shared a certain similarity as "the Golden Children" of the age. F. Scott Fitzgerald was an American, born in Minnesota, educated at Princeton and enjoyed his greatest successes in the mid-20s as the child of the Jazz Age. The Beatles were born in various parts of England and came to flower in the 60s. This course will trace the beginning, middle and concluding periods of their successful years, how they coped with success, the personal setbacks and tragedies and how we can all learn from them.

Related Courses in Literature

The Comic Vision of Henry James, #28145

The Picturesque Novel in the Eighteenth Century, #28738

Was Shakespeare Jewish or Negro? #34020

The Sophomoric Novel of the Deep South, #48025

Novels of the Old West: Works of Rebecca, Morris, Jessamyn and Nathanael West, #67391

The Short Fiction of Short Writers, #90451

French Ticklers: Droll French Farcists of the 20s, #89477

Greek and Roman Dramas that Closed Out of Town, #77394

Furniture and Interior Design in the Modern Novel, #70004

The 10 Best-Dressed Women in Canadian Literature, #70005

Humanities 49

OVER-EXTENSION UNIVERSITY BULLETIN

Philosophy

#17391—IS MAN CONTEMPORARY?
(Fri., 7:30, $25)
Lester Itzbitsky

How contemporary is modern man? This course traces man's contemporariness from the Renaissance to the present day, discussing man's relation to his environment, his social, economic and political problems, his religious beliefs, his customs and rituals, developing the thesis that man was always contemporary with his existing time. The only exceptions were men who were a little behind their time or far ahead of their time. As Mr. Itzbitsky notes, the same holds true for contemporary man today.

#17392—THE INTIMATE LIVES OF FAMOUS PHILOSOPHERS
(Fri., 9:00, $25)
Lester Itzbitsky

This course will portray the more human side of some of our greatest philosophers, uncovering little-known influences on their work that stem from their personal lives—their problems, their loves, their fears and foibles.

You'll learn why Immanuel Kant could not work on Thursdays; how a certain chambermaid changed the course of Hegel's life and how sexual excess nearly destroyed the life of Martin Buber.

This lively, entertaining course will cover the major figures from the sixteenth century to the present, with the emphasis on the Existentialists—the jolly, kite-flying Karl Jaspers, who had to support two imbecile brothers, the secret affair between Camus and Sartre, the childhood accident that nearly traumatized Heidegger and gave him a permanent lisp, and many other colorful, scandalous and inspiring behind-the-scenes accounts of how the great philosophers really lived.

#22222—THE WILD AND CRAZY HUMOR OF JEAN-PAUL SARTRE
(Fri., 7:30, $20)
Ron Brisket

In France, he was also known as "Jean-Paul Satire: Le Roi de Comédie." For the first time, Sartre's zany humor has been translated and published in English. We will analyze Sartre's masterpieces, *How to Be a French-Jewish Mother*, *101 Uses for a Dead Frog*, and *The Frenchie's Handbook*.

#66615—THE MAGIC KEY TO LEARNING ALL PHILOSOPHIES
(Wed., 7:30, $15)
Steve Sapirstein

The Magic Key to all philosophies is explained in Tony's Law, the discovery of Tony LoScalzo, a computer programming student who has devised a formula for deciphering all these works.

"Every philosopher has a section in his work where he gets tired of going around in circles and he just wants to explain his ideas in one short paragraph," said LoScalzo. "My computer programming has come up with the formula for finding this paragraph, or 'sweet spot,' as I call it. You locate the sweet spot and you can zero in on what the guy is trying to say."

Steve Sapirstein, a close associate of Tony LoScalzo, teaches the full version of Tony's Law and all its corollaries and ancillary secrets.

No special knowledge of philosophy is required. Mr. LoScalzo will make a special appearance at the final session to answer questions and explain any of the more difficult philosophical tracts.

Related Courses in Philosophy

Woody Allen: Is He Really Smart or a Psuedo-Intellectual Name Dropper? #19783
The Myth of Myth, #20402
How to Make Money as a Philosopher, #21425
Morbid Preoccupations in Modern Philosophy, #22446
Who Really Killed Jesus? Three New Theories, #21387
Zen Judiasm, #25509
The Total Irrelevance of Hindu Religions, #26524

● BUY A CHARTER MEMBERSHIP IN OUR GOLDEN LIFETIME STUDENT PLAN ●

Take an unlimited number of courses for the rest of your life, all at one astoundingly low price. A once in a lifetime offer! For prices, see Sal, room 443, Mon–Sat, 6 PM to midnight, or call 688-3434.

FASHION

#84732–A HISTORY OF RAINCOATS FROM NOAH TO CALVIN KLEIN
(Tues., 9:00, $30)
Richard Cabrini

It's probably not too farfetched to claim that Noah invented the world's first raincoat. Certainly if he ever ventured out of the ark for only a minute without adequate rain protection he would have been soaked to his skin. We do know that the Hebrews wore a protective coat over their reguair clothes called the *shomar*, which was made of cabbage skins strung together in the form of a long robe. The *shomar* was worn for many years until King Solomon became annoyed with the smell it gave off after long exposure to the warm rains. Being an incredibly wise man, he did not discard the shomar, but instead asked his chefs to devise something edible out of the leaves. Using leftover chopped lamb, pine nuts, onions, raisins and spices they invented stuffed cabbage.

The course will investigate the many forms of the raincoat throughout the ages, concentrating on the sixteenth to the eighteenth centuries, covering the raincoats of the common man and the wealthier classes. We will study actual raincoat samples lent to us by private collectors, including the Elizabethan English *berkin*, made of dried suet, the *swatha*, the Indian royal coat made of carved sandalwood and the beautiful Chinese porcelain bottomless rain urns worn by the emperors and mandarins.

The modern era begins with the invention of the poncho by Pancho Villa. Of course, it was orginally called the "pancho" but was subverted by American mispronunciation. Villa accidentally invented it while engaging in a desperate escape from the Mexican *federales.* He was being smuggled out of prison by one of his aides, wrapped in a large blanket. In the confusion of his escape he tore a hole in the material and put his head through it to see where he was being taken. The hole was exactly in the middle of the cloth and it hung perfectly down to his knees, protecting his body on both sides. He liked the way it looked and wore it constantly, awake and asleep.

The final section of the course is devoted to the modern raincoat styles—the trench coat, the plastic coats and the designer raincoats. A raincoat fashion show is planned for the concluding session.

#47319–THE GOLDEN AGE OF JAPANESE UNDERWEAR
(Thurs., 9:00, $25)
Norris Hunter

The artistic evolution of Japanese underwear reached its peak between the sixteenth and eighteenth centuries beginning with the work of Hatsuhana, through the age of Bunray, Edo, Miyako and up to the late eighteenth-century works of Shusho and Ken. Unlike the western world, the Japanese hold their underwear in the same esteem as their outer garments, reasoning that underwear is the first item of clothing you wear, the most intimate, the closest garment to your skin. Therefore it should be designed with reverence and taste as befitting a person's station in life.

The course will be divided into three sections—royal underwear, the underwear of the upper classes and the simple underwear of the country folk.

Hatsuhana, the first great underwear maker, was also the first to introduce a complete line, garments for both women and men in the various levels of the royal courts. A prince could buy underwear for himself, his wife and his concubines, for both secular and religious affairs. Hatsuhana specialized in bird and fish motifs, working in silks and quilted fabrics. He was especially beloved for his concubine designs including the first known crotchless and bottomless panty, the spider web bra and the teddy.

The men liked to wear loin cloths and molded silk quilting in the same shape as the western "jock." The loin cloth would be hand-painted with the designer's special motifs. Colors would correspond to the "official" colors of the court or the temple or the family.

The designers of the seventeenth and eighteenth centuries created a more complex art—scenes of the royal life, even erotic paintings, which were reserved only for slips and teddys worn by the concubines, which then filtered down to the middle classes as "knock offs" copied by their local underwear designers, who were superb craftsmen in their own right. Ironically, as underwear design became more complex and detailed, the outer clothing became more simplified in line and color, a typical Japanese trait—hiding the complex work under a simple, unadorned facade.

In contrast to the elaborate styles of royalty and the upper classes, both male and female peasants wore simple shorts patterned after early Sumo wrestlers' outfits (our own boxer shorts are derived from this design). They also wore a tank-style undershirt. A simple slit in the front or rear of the wrestler's short took care of elimination. The beauty of peasant underwear was the one simple design motif done in calligraphy by the anonymous craftsmen of the region—a bold slash of black lettering on the neutral background of the linen or flaxen material.

Our two concluding lectures will take place at the Friends of Japan Society where we will see the private underwear collection of the Emperor Hirohito, now on exhibition.

#16847–EXISTENTIALISM AND WOMEN'S FASHIONS
The Influence of Sartre, Camus and Heidegger on Chanel, Balenciaga, St. Laurent, Givenchy and Dior
(Tues., 7:30, $40)
Nita Framboise

The life of the haute couturier, the creator of high fashion in Paris, is far more grueling and difficult than the public ever knows. The French designers especially, must maintain the highest traditions of excellence and creativity in their work if they wish to continue in their position as the natural leaders of fashion and style. One of the most important influences on the French designers have been the Existentialist philosophers who lived in Paris at the same time, especially Sartre and Camus.

The designers were much too busy to actually read the works of the Existentialists. Instead, they would go directly to the philosophers, meet them in a café or for lunch, show them their sketches and ideas and get their advice. Somehow, Camus and Sartre had an uncanny fashion sense, a feeling for what would be popular, both artistically and commercially—and highly competitive, insecure, anxiety-ridden fashion people worshipped and fought over them, outbidding each other for the services of this brilliant pair. It was Sartre who advised Christian Dior to design his famous "New Look," which gave us the long skirt. Camus started St. Laurent on his brilliant early designs such as the trapeze dress. Sometimes one or the other philospher would actually borrow a pencil and draw their own version of the design on a café napkin, which would end up as the final product.

Martin Heidegger worked closely with two early giants of fashion, Chanel and Balenciaga. It was rumored that he was also Coco Chanel's lover. His influence was less specific on Chanel than Sartre and Camus on Dior and St. Laurent, but was more in the general style and spirit of her work. "Heidegger loosened her up," says Nita Framboise. "He gave her the *joie de vivre* that helped her create those wonderful little dresses and suits that revolutionized women's fashion in the 20s and for all time."

Ms. Framboise will show her priceless collection of café napkin sketches and notebook doodles of the philosophers to show how closely they worked with the great designers.

HISTORY

#17760–MINORITY GROUPS IN AMERICA: Why You'll Never Want to Go Back to the Old Country
(Fri., 7:30, $35)
Ben Brith

Why did so many peoples emigrate to the United States from Europe? This course will take us back to the immigrants' homelands and examine their living conditions and motivations for leaving.

Through eyewitness accounts, journals and other original sources, you will learn how rotten things were in Russia, Poland, Austria, Hungary, Romania, Greece, Italy—in fact, in virtually every country in Europe. For the most part, the immigrants had to live in unrelieved poverty, hunger, disease and the constant danger of attack from bigots and bullies.

The second part of the course deals with the same areas of Europe today, how the people are still poor and underfed, how their living conditions are pitiful in comparison with their counterparts in the U.S. The final session will discuss how lucky we are to be living in this country. Mr. Brith will invite everyone to sing the national anthem while he provides musical accompaniment on the accordion.

#69966–HOMOSEXUALS OF THE OLD WEST
(Thurs., 9:00, $45)
G. Arnold Peters

The American homosexual of the nineteenth century shared the same dream as his straight counterparts in our land of opportuniity. He too, made the migration westward in the hope of finding a homestead, a ranch or a new business. He too wanted a piece of the Great American Dream.

Unfortunately, homosexuals had to cope with many problems in order to survive in this cruel, lawless environment. Nearly everywhere they went, homosexuals were ostracized, ridiculed, hated and sometimes murdered. This course will cover the diaspora of the homosexual from the early days of infamy to his hard-won acceptance in California.

We will study the origins of the homosexual ranch lifestyle in Texas, which culminated in the heady atmosphere of the "Gay Caballeros" of El Paso, who along with their employees and friends were brutally murdered in the infamous Ramrod Hill Massacre of 1832. The Gay cowboy of that era was usually a loner, an ex-convict, an army deserter, a drifter who went from job to job. For the most part, he found his sexual partners among the roving Indian tribes, where homosexuals were more prominent. (The legendary Geronimo, the brilliant tribal chief, had many white lovers, including the novelist William Dean Howells and for a brief time on his American tour, Oscar Wilde.)

From the southwest the homosexual made the inevitable move to the far west, to the gold mining towns of Colorado and California. It was there that he found his true calling, in the decorative arts, fashion and business. We will study the emergence of the early Gay lifestyle in California—the colorful Gay bars of the 49'ers, the western boutiques, the leather shops, the first antique and collectibles shops and even an early form of disco that was practiced in Monterrey. One session will be devoted to the pioneering fashion designs of Levi Strauss, a noted homosexual who designed the first "shrink to fit" blue denim jeans for his lover, the infamous Billy the Kid. We will also discuss the colorful lives of other Gay outlaws including the Bruce Brothers, Johnny and Marc, William Weaver and the Other Sons of Katie Elder.

#89170–QUEST FOR BEER AND CIGARETTES
Man's First Experiments with Alcoholic Beverages and Tobacco
(Wed., 7:30, $35)
Maurice Tchaikowsky

As early as 20,000 B.C. Neolithic man was already trying to grow a little food and taste some of the blooming plants around him. Although we cannot place the exact date and place when fermented beverages and tobacco were discovered, we do know from archaeological sources that this early era of mankind was already producing some examples of both kinds of stimulants, as well as keeping them in groups of six and twenty.

This course will explore the more unsuccessful, "amusing" versions of alcohol and tobacco, and in some cases, participate in actual tastings of these early experiments. Some of the beverages to be studied and tasted are Sumerian radish wine, a turnip beer from Mesopotamia, Egyptian beer derived from their sandals, an early form of Vodka made of human hair and a mead made of locust "honey."

#61416–COMMUNISM: MYTH OR FANTASY?
(Wed., 9:00, $25)
Professor Henry Stiff

Professor Stiff proposes the theory that Communism as a political movement and ideology never existed, that what we know and read of this political system is actually an "adversary scenario" originally devised by Franklin Roosevelt during World War II.

In order to maintain economic stability, the so-called Free World needed an enemy—an unfriendly, adversary group of nations that would keep us on a military alert at all times, thus keeping up spending, manufacturing, research and stimulate the economy.

The Russians and other Communist countries were instructed to promote revolutions and general unrest everywhere—thus maintaining a Cold War situation at all times. In return for their "aid" they would receive our technological assistance and foodstuffs.

Aside from a few lapses and unforeseen difficulties and changes in leadership, the "Communists" have followed our orders, according to Professor Stiff. In a brilliant series of lectures, he will trace the evolution of this elaborate scenario (now run by the CIA) to its inevitable conclusion—a future World War which will be in the form of a grudge match between Russia and the U.S., to be waged on a neutral terrain.

#12246–PRIMITIVE CULTURES OF NAKED PEOPLES
(Tues., 9:00, $25)
Harry Markowitz

Comparative studies of selected primitive societies, with emphasis on nude women between the ages of fifteen and twenty-five. We will study in great detail how these women interact with their environment, how their customs have relevance to our own society and its problems. Many rare photographs from *National Geographic* magazine will be shown, in extra-large blow-ups.

#45910–THE IMPACT OF THE SPANISH CIVIL WAR ON COLLEGE FRATERNITIES
(Mon., 9:00, $20)
Christopher Kringle

Many historians contend that the Spanish Civil War was a microcosm of all the political and social forces that have become dominant in our society. Mr. Kringle will discuss how this theory can be applied to college life, especially to the fraternity, which in his terms, becomes "a microcosm of the world not unlike the Spanish War."

Just as the Spanish Civil War was a melting pot for nearly every political and philosophical position, so indeed is the college fraternity. Every fraternity has within itself, the equivalents of the doctrinaire Stalinist, the Trotskyite, the Democratic Socialist, the Christian Democrat, the ultraconservative Fascist, the Liberal Idealist, the Anarchist and the Romantics.

Mr. Kringle draws a brilliant parallel between the warring factions, the rivalries, the nihilism and the blind patriotism of the two phenomena. In conclusion, he will compare excerpts from two famous movies depicting the Spanish War, *This Spanish Earth*, a documentary by Joris Ivens and *For Whom the Bell Tolls*, with the National Lampoon's *Animal House*.

● **EXCLUSIVE MONEY-BACK GUARANTEE IF YOU DO NOT FIND A NEW LOVER** ●

Your tuition fees will be cheerfully refunded if you do not find a new lover in one of your courses.

#28896–GREAT MISTRESSES OF OUR VICE-PRESIDENTS
(Mon., 9:00, $30)
Henry Stiff

A once-neglected area of study that is now causing a significant reinterpretation and revision of many events, thanks to the recent publication of government papers, personal letters and secret documents of our Vice-Presidents. It is now obvious that many Vice-Presidents' mistresses were instrumental in shaping the course of American history.

The course will examine the lives of the mistresses of Martin Van Buren, John Tyler, Teddy Roosevelt, Calvin Coolidge, Harry Truman, and Lyndon Johnson.

A highlight of the course is a study of Tess Truman, the sister of Harry's wife. Bess Truman never mentioned her sister, who was disowned by the family and eventually institutionalized for mental illness and ringworm. But Harry found out about her, and became her ward. As such, he was allowed to take her out for clandestine weekends until she died in 1958. Years later, Truman admitted that he liked Tess primarily because she was simple-minded and easy to take advantage of. "She had no mind of her own," wrote Truman in a recently published letter. "Bess never let me have my way with her. I needed Tess badly, especially when I became President and had all that pressure and important decisions to make. The reason I always slept well and had no qualms of conscience about anything was that I knew that I could release all my tensions and anxieties with Tess.

"Maybe I was a little hard on her—but she did her part for her country and the Free World. On the other hand, I do feel that I owe her an apology for the weekend after Hiroshima. That was a tough week."

Great Mistresses of Our Vice-Presidents is lively, informal history at its best. Although some of our sources are not entirely reliable, we will try to be fair.

Related Courses in History

The Secret Sex Life of the Pilgrim Fathers, #21324
The Pilgrim Mothers, #24485
1001 Horrible Mistakes Made by American Presidents, #27546
The Benevolent Bigot: America's Most Beloved Racists, #86321
Utopian Sports Movements in New England, #69000
Diary of a Slave Laborer in the Pyramids, #67741
Fingernail Paintings of the Mayans, #75155
The North American Indian: Myth or Legend? #18361

CULINARY ARTS

#83617–JEWISH WEDDING AND BAR MITZVAH CUISINE
(Tues., 9:00, $50)
Morris Karpinsky

Anyone who has ever been to a Jewish wedding or bar mitzvah remembers the extraordinary groaning board (or "smorgasbord") of delicious food, food that is only the prelude to the formal dinner but is actually prized and preferred by gourmets in this field. In Jewish wedding cuisine the smorgasbord is actually the showcase presentation where the dazzling gastronomical tour de force is commonplace. This course will teach you how to prepare the same kind of food in your own home, scaling down the ingredients to suit any number of guests.

Morris Karpinsky of the catering firm of Karpinsky and Schraub, will reveal all the tricks of his trade. You'll learn the art of cold cut arrangement, how to carve a turkey and put it back on the frame, how to create your own sculptures in chopped liver (busts of your loved ones, animals, favorite movie stars, etc.), how to create ice fountains of soda and how to make those tasty "hand held" tidbits such as "pigs in blankets," cocktail knishes, miniature egg rolls and other kosher canapés.

In the last session you will go behind the scenes at the elaborate preparation of a real wedding done by Karpinsky and Schraub, picking up invaluable tips "on the job." This is an unusual opportunity to enhance the quality of your food preparation at home, turning your lunches and dinners into exciting catered affairs.

#68120–CHINESE KIMONO CUISINE
(Wed., 7:30, $50)
Elaine Louie

The phenomenal popularity of Chinese cooking continues to grow as food lovers explore the seemingly endless variety of regional cuisines that invade our shores.

After one has mastered the art of Cantonese, Szechuan, Peking, Shanghai and Hunan cooking, the next step is the ultimate one—the exotic, nearly-extinct Kimono cuisine of ancient China. Elaine Louie, a professional chef and an internationally known food expert, will teach an advanced Kimono cooking workshop limited to students who are truly qualified.

No one knows exactly how Kimono cuisine was developed but the popular legend has it that Emperor L'ing T'ang of the Shang Dynasty was bored with the 10,000 odd dishes his head chef could create and in a moment of pique he threw his royal kimono at a servant and demanded that it be prepared as the main course for the evening banquet. The chef (who was no doubt motivated by the possibility of a beheading if he failed to satisfy the Emperor) was inspired, and created the first example of Kimono cuisine—Sweet, Sour, Spicy Breast of Kimono, Double-Steamed and Double-Sauteed, with Eye of Lobster and Nightingale Tongues, Stuffed into Duck Skins and Deep-Fried with Nuggets of Baby Mandarin Persimmons. The Kimono Stuffed Duck Skin was served on the belly of a fourteen-year-old virgin about to become one of the Emperor's concubines.

Today's Kimono cuisine is not as elaborate as Emperor L'ing's and has been adapted for western kitchens without changing its basic qualities. Ms. Louie will teach the fundamental techniques—selection of the proper kimono materials, the various courses and styles of cooking, marinating the kimonos to break the fibers into more edible food, cutting and chopping techniques and the various recipes.

"The best Kimono dishes come from garments that have been worn for years, preferably for generations, so that the body odor of the wearer seeps into the fabric and give the dish a unique taste," says Ms. Louie. Unfortunately, the older, antique kimonos are difficult to find so that the "lived in" taste must be duplicated by wearing it constantly for at least two weeks. "Ideally the wearer should be Chinese," says Ms. Louie. "A kimono worn by a sweaty, meat-eating Caucasian has a heavier, bitter flavor. Chinese perspiration has a more subtle, gentle odor and flavor, with overtones of jasmine and lotus leaves."

Each student will learn how to shop for the proper kimonos, how to prepare complete kimono dinners, including Steamed Kimono Dumplings, Wonderful Taste Kimono, Kimono Foo Young and Eight Precious Kimono Pudding.

#49706–HAIKU AND SASHIMI
(Fri., 7:30, $45)
Melvin Bubblestein

When Sashimi—the Japanese form of raw fish, cut in prescribed form into perfect shapes and eaten in its purest state—and Haiku—the richly suggestive, utterly lyrical and surprisingly rich seventeen-syllable poem—burst upon the American scene, intelligent observers commented that it would only be a matter of time before the two were brought together. Now, Melvin Bubblestein accomplishes that task.

In this course, each student will study the classic haiku, from Basho to Shiki, while eating perfect sashimi provided by a fine local Japanese restaurant. While suitable Japanese music plays in the background, students are encouraged to compress entire meals and complex thoughts into incredible short periods of time, with no sacrifice in quality.

Related Courses in Culinary Arts

Special Recipes for Gay Lovers, #97615
Cooking For No One, #15679
Vintage Years in Diet Sodas, #76159
How to Eat a Pizza #51617
Albanian Country Cooking, #91716

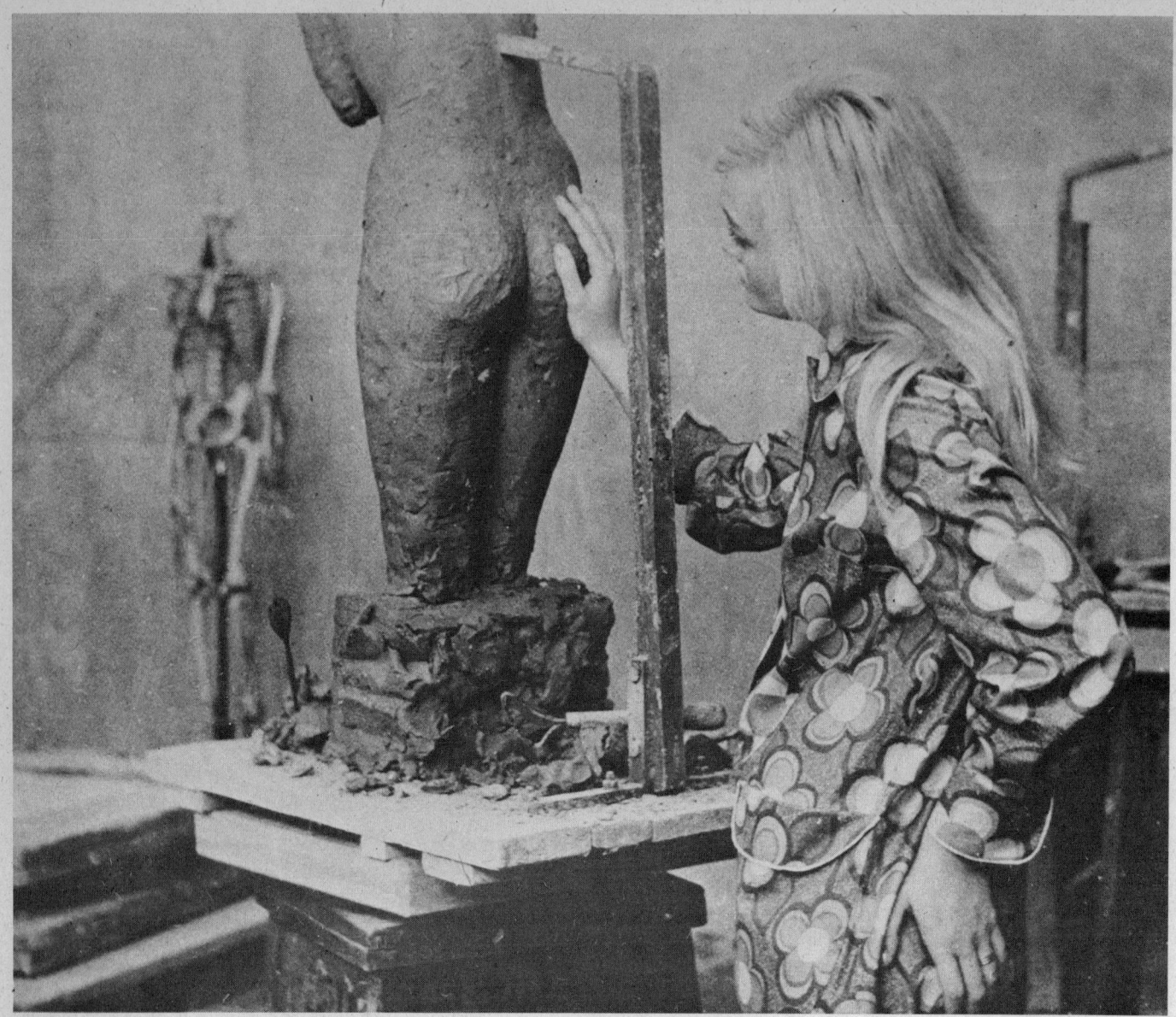

ART

#15947–DECORATIVE PLASTIC STORE SIGNS
(Mon., 9:00, $35)
Marjorie Spalding

Most retail shops are now using plastics as the material for their sign because of its practical qualities. The wood or metal sign is becoming rare, unless it is being used for a specialty store. This course examines the newly discovered decorative treasures in the early versions of the plastic signs, the signs of the 50s and early 60s, before they became a mass-produced product.

Marjorie Spalding, a leading historian in the decorative arts, will show examples and slides from her own collection of early Bakelite, mock Art Deco and mock Moderne signs made during a time when the plastic workers had a respect and curiosity about this new miracle material and tried to adapt their old world traditions to it.

We will also explore the rich, unpredictable world of the naive, primitive plastic store sign, usually designed by "Ma" or "Pa," the owners of Ma and Pa shops. Ms. Spalding will show the marked differences between the small town "Main Street" store signs and the large urban sign. In conclusion we will discuss the future of the plastic sign in shopping centers and highway stores.

#99810–MODERN ART: WHERE IS IT GOING?
(Fri., 9:00, $30)
Rupert Stoones

Today the world of art is more fragmented and chaotic than ever. There are no longer any dominant schools and influences. Buyers are confused, dealers are becoming overly cautious and the public cannot understand much of what is going on. But are there any signs of future trends and movements in all this indecision? Rupert Stoones, associate editor of *Artiste* magazine, discusses what he feels are the three possible waves of the future—animal art, the mono-colorists and nonart art.

"Art is literally going to the dogs," says Stoones. Dog genre painting is attracting many of the younger painters coming right out of school. Cocker spaniels, miniature schnauzers, collies, even bulldogs are the most desired subjects. Dog portraits, dog hunting scenes, dogs and masters, dogs in history, virtually anything to do with dogs will continue to be popular.

Mono-colorists are those painters who do everything in one color, and Mr. Stoones detects a return to dusty pink—such as the dusty pink squares, dusty pink on dusty pink and free-form dusty pink.

The nonart artists are those who do not paint at all and don't even talk about it.

Examples of these three major trends and other mini-trends will be shown and discussed. Mr. Stoones will also present some of the most prominent practitioners of the forms discussed, Steve Schnorr, the dog painter, Billy Zug, the mono-colorist and Andre Gregory, the nonart artist.

#16701–THE ILLUMINATED CHOCOLATE MINATURES OF CHARTRES
(Thurs., 7:30, $25)
Helen Krindelman

One of the most exquisite and awesome works of art created in the Middle Ages was the illuminated chocolate miniatures of the anonymous monks of Chartres. All we know of their identities is that they worked in the back of the cathedral, in one of the small, dusty basement rooms, with little light or ventilation. What emerged is yet another miracle in an art form depicting man's dedication and love of his God.

Only seventy-nine miniatures still survive from what must have been thousands. Each one contains a tiny painting depicting a scene from the New Testament which is illuminated according to secret techniques of the monks and then hand-dipped in a rich homemade chocolate. Somehow, each scene is miraculously clear, right through the chocolate mixture. How the monks accomplished this feat is still unknown, but the latest findings in medieval scholarship deals with a number of theories which will be covered by Professor Krindelman.

#78910–ITALIAN STREET PAINTERS OF THE BAROQUE PERIOD
(Thurs., 9:00, $25)
Giorgio Negroni

The seventeenth- and eighteenth-century Baroque period of Italian art spawned a huge group of painters who worked outside the normal artist-patron arrangement. They worked primarily on the streets of the cities and towns, in cafés, bazaars, street fairs and whenever possible in their own little stalls. Occasionally, if they were lucky or had a minor connection with a prominent family, they could show their works at "patio or courtyard sales."

We will concentrate on the works of three of the most interesting street painters of the time—Giussepe Tortino, the painter of cats with glowing ears, Luigi Caramaggio, a sculptor of homespun family subjects (especially known for his "boys biting their fingernails" series) and Testo Mangiotti, the first street portrait painter who did complete pictures in oils in less than ten minutes.

#21634–THE HANGOUTS OF ITALIAN RENAISSANCE PAINTERS
(Wed., 7:30, $25)
Giorgio Negroni

Almost as important as their painting studios were the cafés and restaurants where the Renaissance painters liked to eat, drink and in the best current style, "hang out." This course studies the great artist's hangouts of the Renaissance and how they influenced the life and works of our greatest painters.

Perhaps the leading café owner of the time was Nunzio Bumbarti, a highly eccentric, colorful entrepreneur who invented the first wine spritzer, "Nunzio's Special," a combination of chianti, sweet vermouth and sparkling mineral water which was used primarily as a laxative. The Café Nunzio was where the major artists of Rome held court, where everyone came to see and be seen, where Michelangelo entertained his friends by drawing hilariously obscene cartoons on the walls and his arch rival Raphael could not even get a table.

● **SPECIAL OFFER** ●
JOIN THE OVER-EXTENSION UNIVERSITY HEALTH & RACQUET CLUB AT LOW INTRODUCTORY RATES!

Enjoy our fantastic health and recreation facilities at remarkably low cost.
- *Beautiful Olympic-style pool*
- *Energy-Saving Low-Heat Sauna*
- *Exercise room featuring chinning bars, mats, mood music, free instruction*
- *Tennis instruction at special low rates from our resident pro, Val Tintindeo.*
- *Aerobic-Disco classes*
- *Snack machines*

And much more! See Miss Nina Scopitone in room 101 for special introductory rates and a guided tour.

Nunzio's main competitor was the Miramar, owned by Alfredo di Napoli, a former baker and confectioner who catered to the notorious sweet tooth of Leonardo Da Vinci, his most illustrious customer. The stories of the Nunzio-Miramar rivalry abound with Italian craftiness and roguery, as they tried to win the other's customers and destroy each other's reputation. Nunzio liked to hire young, starving painters to sit at the Miramar and leave dead rats at the tables. Di Napoli's spies would infiltrate Nunzio's kitchen and substitute salt for sugar and vice versa, making the patrons choke and gag with horror as they ate their favorite dishes. Finally Nunzio challenged Di Napoli to a duel. Michelangelo and Da Vinci served as seconds. The outcome of the duel is probably the most hilarious example of Italian low comedy ever recorded.

The second part of the course will deal with café life in Florence, where a more refined artistic atmosphere prevailed.

Related Courses in Art

How to Buy Art That Matches Your Decor, #12285
Modern Greek-Diner Art, #58221
Scottish Erotic Rubbings, #28521
Van Gogh and Leroy Neiman: The Artist in Torment, #85122

OVER-EXTENSION UNIVERSITY BULLETIN

SPECIAL WEEKEND WORKSHOPS

#05736–THE JOKE-ENDERS WEEKEND
(Fri.–Sun., Dec. 14–16, $60)
Jackie Jerome, Bobby Bee, Lenny Trent

An all-day, all-night intensive weekend workshop designed to help the chronic, obsessed, addicted joke teller. The Joke-Ender Society and Joke-Enders International was developed by Dr. Paul Rabbi, a physician who has successfully cured such comedians as Jack Carter, Pat Henry, Joey Bishop and Corbett Monica from ever telling jokes again. Dr. Rabbi's Joke-Ender therapy sessions have been given all over the country and have worked wonders with professionals and amateurs alike.

The course begins with each participant discussing his problem and how it has degraded his life. Everyone is invited to comment and criticize. If you are tempted to tell a joke you are free to do so, but the rest of the group is encouraged to interrupt, step on your lines, reveal your punch line and otherwise spoil your routine. If, at the end of the day you still have the need to tell a joke you must relate the one the instructor gives you. It will always be an abysmally bad joke, virtually unperformable. But you must tell it to the group, exposing yourself to even greater ridicule. No actual heckling is allowed, since this would encourage new jokes, but you are subjected to bitter, unfunny verbal abuse and even physical harm. By the end of the nonstop weekend marathon most participants are well on the road to the "unjoking" process.

There are three more follow-up classes and then you are invited to a large, convivial party designed to make you go "Cold Turkey." Many of the party guests will approach you in a friendly manner, tempting you with stories and asking you for one of your own. If you weaken at this point you will have the help of your "Straight Man," your specially assigned buddy who steps in during emergencies and immediately destroys any attempt at joke telling. If you pass the Cold Turkey Party you are considered ready to take your place in civilized society, but your Straight Man is always ready to help and can be reached on the special Joke-Ender's "Punch Line" phone.

#57632–THE CONNECTING WORKSHOP
Human Epoxy Techniques for Permanent Bonding
(Saturday, Jan. 9, 2:30, $25)
Seymour Portage

The inability to "connect"—to form a deep, rounded, mature relationship with the opposte sex—is surely one of the most acute problems in modern life. This intensive workshop course teaches the controversial new techniques of using epoxy cement to "bond" yourself permanently to the man of your choice.

Obviously, Human Epoxy Bonding should be used only when you are absolutely certain you want to connect strongly and deeply with a particular person. Otherwise it will be very difficult to separate. It is important to have a thorough preparation, with as much as ten to fifteen years of psychoanalysis or its quasi-professional equivalent approved by your state board of medicine. You must be sure of your emotions and know who you are. In some states, Human Epoxy Bonding cannot be practiced without a note from your analyst.

Basic Human Epoxy is done with the same kind of glues and cements used in carpentry and other work where permanent connecting is necessary. The first part of the course will deal with the particular glue for your needs (the two-part mix, the all in one, the acrylics and the semi-industrial types). After a thorough grounding in the properties of the various glues you will learn the basic connecting or bonding techniques.

The actual technique must be done in a subtle, unobtrusive manner, hiding the area of the body that has the epoxy cement on it. Connecting can be done in the guise of holding your lover's hand, putting your arm around the waist or some kind of similar maneuver—which is called "putting the touch on."

Afterward, you simply squeeze your lover as tightly as possible in the cemented area. This is the important First Bonding Phase. In minutes you should have the beginnings of a permanent connection. While you are in the process of

60 Special Weekend Workshops

bonding you should explain what you've done. This is known as the Asking For a Committment Phase. If your lover says "yes," you pull out the woodworker's clamps you have ready and clamp yourselves as tightly as possible for a few hours for the final bonding. Or, if you can clamp yourselves into a big carpenter's vise you can enter the living together phase. If your lover is hesitant and does not make a committment you can still break the epoxy connection by pulling away from each other as hard as possible.

The second part of the course will discuss the more advanced bonding methods using aircraft and aerospace materials. At this writing, only two states, California and Nevada, permit this technique. These materials can only be used under strict supervision from your doctor because of their near-indestructible qualities.

The final classes will treat the aftermath period. How to disconnect from your lover if the relationship does not work: Some epoxies can be loosened with immersion in paint thinner. Others are more difficult and require intensive treatment and exercises, although magnetic salts and microwave ovens are often effective. Disconnection from aerospace epoxy is extremely difficult and usually requires highly complex laser surgery.

#52143–HOW TO STOP SMOKING—THE TURKISH METHOD
(2 weekends available: Dec. 14–16, Dec. 21–23—Stop Smoking Before Xmas!, $85)
Colonel Nicholas Kebob

The Turks are obsessive smokers of strong, unfiltered cigarettes, which explains why they have one of the highest rates of lung and throat cancer in the world. No matter how hard the public health departments have tried, most Turks have refused to stop this dangerous habit.

In 1980, the mortality rate in Turkey became so alarming that the government medical authorities had to devise a new, fail-safe method to stem the tide of deaths. The method was based on the only psychological motivation the Turkish mind understood—extreme physical torture.

The results were dramatically heartening. Smokers with severe problems were kidnapped and sent to rehabilitation camps where they were tortured by a special branch of the secret police until they agreed to stop smoking forever. In the first 125,000 cases, all were successful, and eventually everyone was allowed to return to a normal life.

The method is especially appealing to those for whom lectures on the evils of tobacco, behavior modification, and special filtration devices have proven useless. The Turkish Method is based on the premise that in order to smoke a cigarette you have to put it in your mouth and light it with your hands. The torture techniques concentrate on these areas. You are allowed to smoke as much as you like throughout your stay. The smoker learns, however, that continued smoking only encourages continued torture.

The phases of the torture are as follows:

(1) The lips are "stretched" into useless tissue.
(2) The lips are removed.
(3) The teeth are removed with pliers.
(4) The tongue is removed.
(5) The fingers are removed at the rate of one a day, followed by the rest of the hand.

If anyone wishes to smoke after this he is free to do so. His condition is considered hopeless and he is sent home. It was discovered that only a hardened few would even submit to Phase One of the Method. In any case, everyone in the camp is brutally sodomized before leaving, to instill an extra sense of self-discipline, pride and self-preservation.

Colonel Nicholas Kebob, formerly with the Istanbul Secret Police, conducts a modified version of the Turkish Program for American smokers. Instead of complete removal of the lips, tongue, teeth and hands, he uses "gradual aggravation," the slow burning of these vital organs with lighted cigarette butts. He also recommends sodomizing for extra discipline.

Note: This is a purely voluntary program designed for hardcore smokers with severe health problems. We maintain no responsibility for its outcome, nor any of the possible side effects that could be entailed.

#91320–PORN MOVIE WORKSHOP
(Jan. 9–11, $150)
Guy DeBono

One of the most productive areas for aspiring filmmakers promises to be the adult X-rated movie, especially for cable TV. This course takes you from the basics of porn filmmaking right up to the production of a feature film, covering all aspects and contingencies.

First, you will learn how to shoot the 8mm "loop" and the five to ten minute short will help you master the basic set-ups, the various positions and physical match-ups. You will learn how to shoot the "insert" shots, the "piston" technique, how to use a slow camera pan, extreme close-ups, overhead shots and much more.

From 8mm loops we go directly into 35mm feature film production as you will make your own film. You will learn how to arrange for financing, how to budget a film, how to advertise and audition for talent, how to choose the right actors and actresses, how to use the "casting couch" productively, how to write a successful script, how to use advanced photographic and lighting techniques, how to encourage improvisation. All areas of post-production will be covered, including distribution.

In each phase of the course you will work with professional writers, performers and directors to pick up invaluable knowledge in this highly promising film field—tips covering the proper use of ice cubes and warm water, simulating the real thing, using visual symbols and creating exciting effects through editing. You will discover how to borrow and adapt story ideas from existing legitimate films. (*A Star is Porn, Raiders of the Lost Dork, Dr. Strangesex*). The final area of discussion will be how to write catchy advertising, with the porn publicist Bernie Brillbroad, who wrote the award-winning headline for *"The Man Who Came At Dinner"* ("You Need a Handkerchief for This Film . . . But Not For Your Tears.")

Special Weekend Workshops 61

FACULTY BIOGRAPHIES

BORIC ABRAHAMS has a Ph.D. from Vanessa University in noncomparative literature. He is a noted Kafka scholar specializing in the great novelist's most personal, intimate affairs.

BARRY BEAVERMAN is a graduate of Oxford U. of Indiana where he majored in social interaction and family recreation. He runs a successful party planning service for basement owners.

TANYA BECK holds seven degrees in anthropology and physical therapy and is the leading living authority on Tibetan nostril massage.

BOBBY BEE has been a comedian, a joke-writer, a dry cleaner, a butcher's assistant, a tree surgeon and Under-Secretary of State for Costa Rica.

MARTY BERNIE is a leading independent producer of films whose credits co-include *Sunset Boulevard II*, *The Tiger's Revenge*, *Pardon My English* and *Vegetable House*.

GORDON BIBBELING is a specialist in overeating.

WENDY BIBBELING holds a degree in Semiotic Semantics from Nylon University and specializes in communicating with herself.

PROFESSOR MORRIS BLUESTEIN is a specialist in Hasidic Ballroom Dancing and teaches at Yeshiva Tech. His book, *Dance, Jew, Dance!* has recently won the Eli Mendelthaler Award.

BARBARA BOGASH holds a B.A. in Fashion Technology from the Kenilworth School of Design. She is a consultant to a leading designer jean company and will soon be introducing her own line of color coordinated checkbooks.

HELEN BOGASH holds a number of degrees in Life Crises and Turning Points. She has been studying the midlife crises of the Moroccan Berber for twenty-eight years.

SHELLY BOGASH, Executive Director of Smoke Detectors, Unlimited, is also the President of Imperial Dressed Beef Corporation and is on the board of Capitol Printing and Engraving Co.

IVOR BONEYARD is the Director of the Mighty Thespians of Thor Playhouse, the oldest, all-lisping acting troupe in the country.

RON BRISKET is a freelance writer and editor specializing in French Existentialist humor. His latest article, *The Bisque Belt: Fear and Trembling on the French Riviera Circuit*, appeared in *Shtique* magazine.

BEN BRITH is the Director of the Ben Brith Company, an organization dedicated to promoting the American Way of Life.

BETTY BROWNAPPLE has spent a lifetime researching the differences between various kinds of salt. Her work has taken her from the mines of Siberia to the ultramodern factories of Morton and Diamond Crystal.

TED BROWNROSE is a close associate of Norman Tremble, author of *Six of One, Half a Dozen of the Other: The "V" Theory of Negotiation*. He is the only authorized teacher of the theory.

MELVIN BUBBLESTEIN is a Professor of Japanese Fish and Poetry at Bogart College.

BARRY BUGMAN, a professional stand-up comedian, is a student of Third World comedy and has brought over many exiciting comedy acts from Africa and Asia. He has played every major room in Kenya, Togo and Nigeria.

MANUEL BUICK is a Professor of Grotesque Literature at Norbert College. His articles have appeared in *Splinters*, *The Moth* and the *Norbert Quarterly*.

G. MURRAY BUMBARDO is an internationally famous liquor and wine drinker who specializes in offbeat, new wines from Asia and Africa. His nickname is "Spud."

JAY BUMBARDO is an expert on breaking into movie houses and watching the film for nothing. He is now a security consultant for a leading theater chain.

SEYMOUR BUPP has done a thorough job in investigating all the ways you can bathe and shower properly and wants to share them all with you.

JOANNA BUSHING is a freelance inventor and illustrator of children's books.

BOB BUSHMEYER is an expert on minute meats and has submitted many articles to *Meat and Meat By-Products* and *Kosher Butcher* magazines.

RICHARD CABRINI writes popular history and general interest articles for many magazines and has just made a three-story deal with *Buzz* magazine.

RIP CARVER is a freelance carpenter and handyman who is a consultant nostalgia party planner for those who must revive the spirit of the 60s and 70s.

CARMINE CASALAQUA is an expert on teaching criminally gifted children and criminally gifted adults.

SPENCER COLON is an expert on buying personal stationery wisely and economically. He has written many pieces for *Pad and Pen*, the stationer's trade magazine.

GUY DEBONO is one of the leading directors of 8mm porn loops and theatrical porn features. His latest films are *Take My Wife . . . Please* and *A Roman Springs on Mrs. Stone*.

ARTHUR DIBRODO is an assistant professor of Romance Languages at Breakstone University. Next summer he will offer a six-week Chinese restaurant tour through Italy and Greece.

BRUCE DIMPLER, B.S., has a hard-won degree in para-psychology and ceramics from Gaylord Tech.

GARY DIMPLE, formerly Vice-President of the Vinnie Carbonara Stock Broker Investment Company now writes and publishes *The Dimple Line*, a newsletter for $1 to $5 portfolios. He is also a licensed private investigator, specializing in matrimonial problems.

BONNIE DITZ, sister of Sandy Ditz, is a professional street mime who specializes in double-jointed "finger tricks." She has performed all over the globe and her one-woman show "Ditzy Fingers" received an "Arny" Award from the National Critics Association.

SANDY DITZ, sister of Bonnie Ditz, runs her own sandwich shop and is one of the nation's premier avant-garde sandwich makers. Her shop, Sandy's Sandwich Shop, is frequented by many celebrities in cable TV.

JANICE FLANNEL has made a lifelong study of the effectiveness of various detergents, waxes and polishes on furniture surfaces. She is a cum laude graduate of Tarbell College.

NITA FRAMBOISE is a fashion and furnishings writer for many newspapers and magazines and specializes in French Existentialist contributions to haute couture.

NINA GINGLIA is the head sandwich chef at Val's Luncheonette. She has taught sandwich making at various workshops at home and abroad and recently won a Golden Pickle at the International Sandwich Festival in Cannes.

BERNICE GROOBER is the author of *How to Save Thousands a Year with Teeth Manicures*, a creative approach to nail biting.

STAN GROOVER is the owner, along with his wife Vicki, of Stan and Vicki's Leather and Cheese Shop, a store that sells custom-made leather clothing that uses ornate cheese decorative trim.

GREGOR HAKI is one of the Grand Masters of *Yevti* or Turkish Towel Snapping. He has won many national and international championships and now teaches the short stroke and coil method.

MYRON HANKER is a leading writer and consultant on men's fashions, specializing in belts and suspenders. He is

Faculty Biographies

introducing his own line of convertible belt/suspenders in the near future.

LEONARD HAYMISH is a TV critic and humorist who writes for many newspapers, magazines and scholarly journals. He is currently writing a critical study of Gary Coleman.

NORRIS HUNTER, P.A. Stromberg University, BLT, Hayward Tech., teaches Japanese Lingerie History at Parnes University.

LESTER ITZBITSKY is the Chairman of the Philosophy Department of Spooner College. His annual seminar on Contemporary Man attracts many important people.

JACKIE JEROME has been a stand-up comedian since the age of two. He specializes in comical music routines on the saxophone and teaches comedy at Ed-Mart Junior College.

BARNEY JERSKI is a retired bartender and veteran beer drinker who has never spilled an ounce of beer on anyone in fifty-two years of pouring and serving.

BERNARD JUGULARSKY is an expert on animal law and the legal rights of domesticated trained animals. He has represented Lee Marvin, Ernest Borgnine, George Kennedy and Curt Jurgens in dog-imony suits.

MORRIS KARPINSKY is the head of the catering firm of Karpinsky and Schraub. He teaches Haute Bar Mitzvah Cuisine at the American Temple of Gastronomy.

SEYMOUR KARTEL is a CPA whose avocation is finding the best cookie bargains in the city. His investigations and numerous articles have made him the number one cookie "maven" in the country. He is also an authority on how to make long-distance phone calls.

COLONEL NICHOLAS KEBOB is a former member of the Turkish secret police who specializes in mind-alteration and creative pederasty.

LANISLAW KELB is a brilliant amateur botanist specializing in the secret life of unborn plants.

BARNEY KITZEL is a beloved jazz and R & B historian who has done more to popularize the work of obscure local musicians than anyone in his field. He is the author of *Hog Mouth: The Biography of Ernest "Hogmouth" Tibbs*, the quadriplegic harmonica player, and has a monthly column in *Riff* magazine.

HYMAN KLAU is the country's foremost authority on quack medicine and new frontiers of healing. He has lectured everywhere and is the author of *Why a Quack? A History of Para-Normal Medicine*.

SOLOMON KLIPSPRINGER is Jewish and a licensed real estate dabbler. He has picked up a lot of useful information from friends and is a potential expert in this field.

JACK KNORFMAN has retired from active life at the age of twenty-one and is now teaching many others to do the same.

BRUCE KOGL is the sole owner and President of Bruce Kogl Enterprises, a leading purveyor of "scratch 'n' sniff" products.

YAKAMOKO KON is the popularizer of the new Japanese martial art, *Sony*, the art of self-defense using battery operated small appliances. Mr. Kon also teaches other methods that use larger objects, including Yamaha, Sansui, Mitsubuishi and Honda.

SEYMOUR KREML owns the Seymour Kreml Unisex Hairdressing Salon and is the creator of a new line of men's toiletries called "Epar" (Rape, spelled backwards).

HELEN KRINDELMAN is a Professor of Miniature Art at Elfinore University and has published many books in her field.

CHRISTOPHER KRINGLE is the pioneer theorist and developer of Body Odor Language. He is Visiting Professor of Body Odor Language at Splendid Junior College.

LAWRENCE KUGL was once a highly promising trial lawyer and now still practices at the Louis Brandeis Legal Flea Market. Mr. Kugl is currently writing *A Guide to Lawyer's Flea Markets* in America along with his associate, the professional haggler, Tufti Halva.

MURRAY LAPEL has had many years of experience working for an optician, and has developed a foolproof patented method for finding missing contact lenses.

LARRY LASEUR is a hair stylist at Mr. Ben's Hair City. He has also appeared on the *Hair Today, Hair Tomorrow* TV show.

VICTOR LASZLO is a filmwright and former leader of the Free French Underground in World War II. He is currently writing a musical about the life of Charles De Gaulle.

ELAINE LOUIE is a professional chef and internationally known food expert who specializes in highly exotic Chinese cuisine. Her newest work, *Cooking with Opium* will be published very soon.

LARRY LUCCIONE is a former bartender, ballroom dancer and state senator who is an expert on singles' dating styles and the various "hot centers" where the best catches can be found.

GEORGE LUNGER, a T.M.A. from Huddleston College, teaches conceptual relationships in the arts at Breakstone University. His latest book, *Words, Music, Pictures and Buildings*, will be published soon.

JOHN MANDARINI is the author of *Vic Damone: An Unauthorized Biography*. He is a scholar of the modern-day pop crooner. His Ph.D thesis *Perry Como and the Cardigan Sweater in Musical Fashion* is a landmark in musical criticism.

PETE MANILLA has long devoted himself to the history of Greek jazz, and is the world's only living authority on the subject. He has taught Greek jazz at Bunion College, Yeshiva Tech. and the University of Sierra Leone.

TED MANN teaches many courses in clam shucking and lobster boning at gourmet societies and cooking clubs.

MICHAEL MARCEAU is the creator of the Word Mime Workshop, a combination of words, mime, dialogues and song. He is no relation to Marcel Marceau.

HARRY MARKOWITZ teaches many courses on the cultures of primitive societies and is an expert in the use of slide projectors.

LEW MASTERSON has had years of experience in the service franchise field and is currently developing a line of college-oriented businesses called "fast fad" franchises.

STEVEN MENSCHEVIK is a starving writer of fiction who has yet to publish a book. He is colorful, witty and an interesting dinner companion, but is highly allergic to shrimp.

GIORGIO NEGRONI teaches Italian art at Bontempo Junior College and is co-owner of a hairdressing salon in Naples.

DR. MARVIN J. NICKSTEIN is a former executive with the NASA Program who has discovered many forms of life on other planets. He has lectured at Kranis University, Bernard College and the Festival of Lights in Milwaukee.

DR. FRANK NIDELINGER is an internationally known cheese collector. He is Associate Editor of *Curds and Whey* magazine and lectures on antique cheese at Chalfont State.

RINALDO NOVOLUCCI, one of the most acclaimed directors of the modern cinema, is currently at liberty and is ready to accept any suitable project worthy of his talents and stature.

TOMMY O'CALLAGHAN is a professional beggar with a reputed six-figure income, a condominium in New Mexico and a houseboat on the Thames.

GEORGE PACHINKO has a B.S. in Criminal Investigation from Menemsha College and has lectured in over thirty states on how to convert serious voyeuring into a professional career in criminal surveillance.

G. ARNOLD PETERS, B.A., M.A. Carson University, lectures on offbeat subjects for many schools, clubs, and business organizations.

LOUIS PINTCHEK teaches alchemy at Nathan K. Brandberberg University. He has the largest collection of gold in the world.

SEYMOUR PORTAGE is a specialist in human inter-relations, with a degree from Brundage U. He is a frequent contributor to *Feelings* magazine.

JEFFREY PUSHBERG is the author of *Stop, Look and for God's Sake, Listen*, a guide to speed listening.

JACK PUTRELL is one of the nation's leading authorities on novelty t-shirts. He owns one of the largest collections in this genre and has donated many shirts to museums, galleries and corporate headquarters for exhibition.

MAX RESNICK has an academic degree from Bogart High School and has attended Susquatch Junior College for three years. He is an expert on corporate security guarding and long-range voyeuring.

FRANK ROSE is a prominent popular music critic and social historian who has managed to convey an accurate portrait of the music scene without compromising himself.

EGBERT ST. JOHN is a film historian and critic whose most recent work is *The Black Homosexual in Film*.

RAFAEL "SKULL" SANCHEZ was formerly deputy warlord of the Satin Baboons, one of the most feared street gangs in the city. He has given guided tours of his slum neighborhood to intrepid adventurers and has also appeared on many local TV news shows.

STEVE SAPIRSTEIN is a disciple and close associate of Tony LoScalzo, the inventor of Tony's Law: the Key to Learning All Philosophies.

NINA SCARF a graduate of the Dreydil School of Music, teaches piano and accordion to gifted animals and slightly retarded humans.

ROSS SCHINGLEBURGER has done considerable work with senior citizens in muscle control and organ rejuvenation. He is currently Masseur-in-Residence at Quill College.

JACK SCHVITZER is the sales manager of Jack 'n Jay's Appliances. He has a personal collection of over 500 clock radios, which are set to go off at the same time.

HILDA SCROFULA author of *Can I Borrow a Cup of Dinner for Life?* is the nation's leading authority on food borrowing for survival. Ms. Scrofula has not paid for any of her own meals for the past thirteen years.

PEPI SCUMBAZZO is the head truck driver of a garbage carting service specializing in collecting from late-night restaurants, bars, discos and after-hours clubs. His unique Midnight Garbage Carting Tour has won the Oscar Trowbridge Award for Creative Tourist Entertainment from the American Travel Agents Association.

GREG SHAYMUS holds a B.S. in Sports Shoe Medicine from Poplin College. He is a consultant to the Cheetah Shoe Company of Bulgaria as well as a Grand Dragon of the Loyal Order of Hypnotists.

T. WALKER SIBLEY, a graduate of Bonaparte University, is one of the world's experts in coal miner's songs, chants and hollers.

MURRAY SKIRMISCH is a dedicated opera goer and critic who always falls asleep after the first act and wakes up for the third. He has lectured on staying awake at the opera to many audiences and tours regularly for the government.

MARJORIE SPALDING is a popular art historian with many friends and owns a superb collection of early plastic store signs.

JAY SPECK owns one of the largest collections of collectibles in the country, including a 1942 pizza takeout box.

LEONARD SPICKE teaches mathematics at the Ariel Free College and Maynard Jarvis University. He also has his own math show on many FM radio stations.

MYRON SPITTSBARD has worked in many areas of research and marketing and is now head of his own consultant firm, The Spittsbard Group.

NUNZIO SQUIGLIANTI is an expert in the evaluation of the criminal potential in children.

PROFESSOR HENRY STIFF is a psychotherapist with an extensive practice who makes a good living. He has many satisfied patients who have been with him for years.

LEONARD STOONES is a maitre d' in one of the city's finest restaurants and has given many courses in how to greet people and shake their hands properly. He has also advised many of our leading politicians on how to cure sweaty palms.

RUPERT STOONES is Associate Editor of *Artiste* magazine and a leading critic of modern art. He has just written and produced a TV mini-series on the lost sculptures of Boris Minnevitch.

URBNIAK SVEVO, the son of Ladniak Svevo, continues in his father's tradition by producing and directing the internationally famous Svevo Living Puppet Theater of Latvia.

ICHIKO TARASAWA is a Black Hanky in H'ai L'ai, the Japanese martial art of trembling and fear. He has studied at many famous schools and now has his own cable TV show, the Ichiko Tarasawa Show.

MAURICE TCHAIKOWSKY is a noted social anthropologist who specializes in man's early quest for alcohol and tobacco products.

MARIA TEDESCO has made over a million dollars by stuttering effectively and intimidating people.

HAL TINSLEY is an amateur beekeeper who has been successful using unorthodox methods which are described in his best-selling volume, *1001 Bees in a Box*.

SEYMOUR TOKAY is one of the world's leading authorities on the proper way to scratch your body.

HENRY C. TONNAWAY has been in the cable business for over thirty-five years and specializes in heavy-duty black cable with the rubberized casing, usually wound around huge wood spools.

I. PHILLIP TORTONE is a dealer and writer in antiques and collectibles, specializing in food wrappers and non-recyclable plastic.

LENNY TRENT conducts his own radio comedy talk show on WLRT, a cable radio show supported by listener contribution.

PAUL TRINKLER is one of the pioneers in modern dance and ballet. His choreographic style is based entirely on insect behavior patterns.

NORMAN TRUEBERGER is an urban planner and a wine expert. He holds degrees from Pomander College, Farney Tech, Killgore U. and Rathbone State Teachers.

HUGH TUNGWELL teaches the modern American novel at Engelheisen University. His standard work, *How to Read a Read* re-evaluates and elevates the works of Sidney Sheldon, Judith Krantz and many others to their rightful niches in American literature.

NORMAN TURLMAN is a graduate of the Bona Fide School of Hotel Management and is currently the owner-manager of the Matinee Motel Chain.

DONNA TWIDZIK has spent years instructing people in how to meet unusual new lovers, and owns one of the biggest Roll-A-Dex files in the country.

STANLEY VERMIN writes a weekly column on semiclassical music for the Bruce family syndicate of newspapers. He is a graduate of the Fulcrum School of Music and Haber College.

ARMAND VON LIMBO has developed many small businesses and has kept them small. His specialty is developing small businesses.

MAURY WAFTEL is President of ACI, American Cottage Industries, a franchiser in cottage building. He was the developer of Little Village, a retirement community for midgets.

MAURICE WAKAMBA was Lifetime President of Chad for three days but was forced to abdicate when teenage rebels stole his car. He is currently raising funds for a counter-revolution.

HARVEY WALL is a professional taster and chewer for one of America's largest gum manufacturers. He is a charter member of the Societe de Tastevin de Gum.

MARC WINSLOW is President of Gays in Computer Programming (GCP), a non-profit organization devoted to solving the problems of gays in computer programming.

BARNEY ZINGARA has spent many years in Africa absorbing the atmosphere of the big game hunting safaris and owns a gun license for both small and large arms.

MAX ZOROASTER was formerly an assistant manager of a Safeway store in Buffalo, New York and has shopped in supermarkets for many years.

DR. PAUL ZUGSMITH is the founder of the "Hello, How's Your Hole . . ." Family Clinic and a frequent contributor to underground psychiatric journals.

JACK ZWIGMAN, a graduate of Lorimar Tech, teaches off-the-wall, far-out conceptual art. He is currently completing a paint-by-number conceptual art kit for mass market distribution.